Living Modern:

Living Modern:
A Biography of
Greenwood
Common

Waverly B. Lowell

WILLIAM STOUT
PUBLISHERS

RICHMOND, CALIFORNIA

This book was published with the assistance of
The Getty Foundation,
the Graham Foundation for Advanced Studies
in the Fine Arts,
and the LEF Foundation.

Published in cooperation with the
College of Environmental Design,
University of California, Berkeley

Berkeley / Design / Books promote historical and
critical scholarship on subjects drawn from the
Environmental Design Archives at the University
of California, Berkeley. One of the nation's premier
design archives, its collections hold graphic materials,
written documents, and personal papers concerning
American and foreign architecture, landscape
architecture, and planning.

Marc Treib, Series Editor
Waverly Lowell, Archives Curator

Published by
William Stout Publishers
1326–1328 South 51st Street
Richmond, California 94804
www.stoutpublishers.com

Printed in China

Dedicated to the residents
of Greenwood Common

Part 3:

The Houses

Introduction

The hills of north Berkeley, California, are rife with residences that range in form from homey, shingled Arts-and-Crafts bungalows to quaint, period revival houses to starkly modern examples from the postwar period. John Galen Howard, architect of the Beaux-Arts plan for the University of California, Berkeley, and founder of its architecture program, lived there. So did the architect Bernard Maybeck, a leader in the region's Arts and Crafts movement, and there he built some of his most famous houses: the Andrew C. Lawson house (1907), the Charles C. Boyton house, known as the Temple of Wings (1912), and the Alma Kennedy house and music studio (1914), as well as his own 1909 home.

Maybeck also responded to the problems linked to hillside living. Following the devastating fire of 1923, which roared west down the Berkeley Hills and destroyed a substantial portion of residential north Berkeley, he promoted the use of "bubblestone," a fireproof aerated concrete for cladding buildings. He used it on the home he built to replace the one lost in the fire.[1]

After World War II the area became home to growing numbers of white-collar, middle-class professionals, particularly those associated with the nearby University of California. Among the other residents who moved to the Berkeley Hills during the 1950s were the architect William Wilson Wurster, dean of the University of California's School of Architecture, and his wife Catherine Bauer Wurster, city planner, educator, and author. They had only recently moved to Berkeley from the Boston area. Their move lies at the foundation of Greenwood Common.

Wurster's Cambridge colleagues included leading architects and landscape architects who had begun to think about the new communities adjacent to cities that would develop in the aftermath of World War II. The nation's changed demographics led to a more urban national identity and centralized employment districts. These in turn resulted in a dramatically increased need for housing in or near cities. The availability of undeveloped land permitted designers and developers to circumvent planning the innovative new towns then being developed in a recovering Europe, new towns such as Stevenage in Great Britain (1946) and Vällingby in Sweden (1954). Instead they pursued a more dispersed, suburban approach to building future communities.

However, like their counterparts in Europe, these designers were also committed to an aesthetic that employed the modernist paradigm and new materials promoted in Europe before the war. These promising new suburban developments included Snake Hill, developed by the architect Carl Koch in Belmont, Massachusetts, in the early 1940s; Six Moon Hill, in nearby Lexington, planned by The Architects Collaborative (TAC) in 1950, and Hollin Hills in Fairfax, Virginia, with Dan Kiley as landscape architect (1950).

On the West Coast, architect Gregory Ain worked with landscape architect Garrett Eckbo to design a number of communities in southern California such as Mar Vista Housing in Los Angeles (1948–49) and Park Planned Homes in Altadena (1947).

Eckbo, with his partner Robert Royston and architects John Funk and Joseph Stein, also worked in northern California on the planning of Ladera, a development for the Peninsula Housing Cooperative in Palo Alto (1948).[2] These developments were based on a social philosophy of community in conjunction with a modernist design aesthetic that included preferences for natural materials and a sensitivity to regional climate. Their plans also reflected a particular lifestyle that rendered them different from other new suburbs such as the Levittowns springing up on the east coast and elsewhere that seemed to pursue quantity rather than quality. The intent of those developments was twofold: to provide housing and to generate profits. These endless rows of limited façade, cookie-cutter houses were sold to working-class and newly middle-class families. They were not constructed within any broader social context or design philosophy, and they were managed by development companies.

In contrast, Six Moon Hill was intended to provide homes for the TAC architects themselves, but their idea of an architecturally integrated community of modest, affordable houses also appealed to academics and other professionals in Cambridge. They believed that a community based on cooperative governance, good site planning, and harmony of design would serve as an antidote to the monotony of most Federal Housing Authority-financed neighborhoods.[3]

At Snake Hill, Carl Koch's modernist exteriors created a homogenous neighborhood managed by the owners as a corporate entity controlling the land and infrastructure. At Hollin Hills, Charles Goodman and developer Robert Davenport—with landscape architects Dan Kiley, Lou Bernard Voigt, and Eric Paepcke—

built a carefully considered community of houses with interior spaces that flowed into the landscape. The grounds of each home, they believed, should merge with the next to create a park-like setting.[4] And of the projects planned by Eckbo and his partners, most were envisioned as modernist enclaves for people with shared values.

William Wurster was aware of all of these projects being undertaken by his friends and colleagues when he began to plan Greenwood Common in Berkeley. Unlike these other projects, which were being developed on twenty or more acres, the tract for the Common consisted of only two-and-a-half acres. Wurster took full advantage of the limited space when he envisioned a development that combined an idealistic sense of community with a modernist aesthetic and an awareness of regional traditions. It was to feel more like a small village than a large town.

It is only natural that Greenwood Common has been compared to a New England village green, a common, a town square, a bungalow court, New York's private gated Gramercy Park, and even a planned unit development (PUD).[5] All of these references embrace a group of buildings set in relation to a planted or paved central area open to the public. But all of those comparisons are either too superficial or too grandiose for the small community of houses that today comprise Greenwood Common. Yes, it is a cluster of residences surrounding a semipublic green area—but it is not restricted, has none of the commercial or institutional entities of a village green or town square, nor the PUD's possibilities for multiplication.

At Greenwood Common, the green space and the views across the San Francisco Bay to the Golden Gate prevail. It exists as a utopian oasis in the crowded Berkeley Hills; where neighbors share the expanse of lawn, hold family picnics, watch their children frolic, play with their dogs, and celebrate weddings and other special events. Ironically, the lawn was not part of the original plan; only a small part of the initial design was assigned to shared outdoor space. A pair of lots occupied the center of the site, but these were—quite fortunately—never built upon, and they have become the ground on which the history of the Common has been painted.

It is these two lots that serve as a reminder of the blackberry fields and groves of Monterey pines that no longer grow there, and of the Berkeley Hills with their expansive views to the bay and beyond. The expectation of two homes on these lots explains the plum allée, why the houses on the north side of the lawn were fenced, and why the houses on the south side of the central green area face away from the Common. Only one house has large areas of glass that open onto the Common, the Maenchen House; it alone was planned to face the smaller open space originally proposed.

William Wurster purchased the land and developed the property. It has been said that he encouraged, some say cornered, young academics to buy his lots. Most taught at the University of California and those who did not knew Wurster in some other capacity. The actual degree of Wurster's involvement in the selection of architects and site planning is a matter of conjecture, but it is clear he was an active participant.

Greenwood Common's nomination as a subject for one of the Berkeley/Design/Books was an obvious choice. The Common is special in the way it occupies its site, in its identity as a cluster of homes around a semiprivate park, and for the vision that created it. Eight distinct homes—designed for different owners by eight significant California architects—harmonize effortlessly with each other and with their site. It captures what had become the mid-century ideal of indoor-outdoor living and the Wursters' belief that to thrive families and communities need both public outdoor space and private outdoor space.

Of the eight architects involved in its development, the Environmental Design Archives holds the records of six. Most were well known at the time and had carved out reputations on the West Coast, although they merited greater national recognition. Two had international reputations by the time the Common was developed. These were William Wilson Wurster, noted for residential design and his role as dean of Berkeley's School of Architecture, and Harwell Hamilton Harris, with a national reputation as an architect and dean of the architecture school at the University of Texas.

The others were Joseph Esherick, John Funk, Henry Hill, Robert Klemmedson, Howard Moïse, and Donald Olsen. The landscape of Greenwood Common was designed by Lawrence Halprin, who also designed gardens for four of its homes. Geraldine Knight Scott designed another of the gardens while the other three were created by their architect or homeowner.

Because each client, architect, and design was unique, the stories of the houses and their gardens are also unique. That some stories are longer than others is due to the quantity, content, and type of records available for study. This book is both an architectural and social history of an uncommon place and a community. It presents a tapestry woven of stories spun by personalities, talents, intersecting lives, family needs, and economics. It is a biography not of a person but of a place.

Waverly B Lowell
January 2009
Berkeley

All the projects discussed in the text are located in California, unless otherwise noted.

Acknowledgments

First and foremost I gratefully thank all of the current residents of Greenwood Common: Robert Birge, Laura Schaaf, Katinka and Fred Wyle, SB Master and James Symons, Joan McDonough, Elliot Porter, Frances Burnett, and Dan and Kate Funk, who graciously spoke with me and generously gave of their time. They invited me into their homes, responded to my numerous questions, lent me photographs, told me stories, and provided me with five decades of minutes from the Board of Directors of Greenwood Common, Inc.

Thanks to Lawrence Halprin, Donald Olsen, Robert Klemmedson, James Ackerman, Richard Vignolo, and Gio Morse who shared memories of their involvement with the Common, and to Joshua Baer and Sadie Super for providing documentary materials and encouraging their use. A special note of gratitude to Matthew Güereña who kindly shared his talent, skills and time to create clear and readable plans and to Cris Benton who braved sun, wind, and rain to take splendid photographs from above.

I owe a great deal to all of my colleagues in the numerous archives across the country who assisted me with locating and reproducing the documents and images that add to an understanding and appreciation of Greenwood Common: William Whitaker at the University of Pennsylvania, Kurt Helfrich at the University of California, Santa Barbara, Beth Dodd and Nancy Sparrow at the University of Texas, Austin, and Christine Bunting and Patrick Haywood at the University of California, Santa Cruz.

Numerous individuals from the College of Environmental Design have participated in this endeavor in a variety of ways. Jan Miller of the Dean's Office allowed me to take time to work on the book, Elizabeth Byrne, Head Librarian of the Environmental Design Library, located obscure and not-so-obscure reference sources; Miranda Hambro, Assistant Curator of the Environmental Design Archives, assisted in managing reproductions and displaying great patience with records left unfiled during my research; and Steven Brooks, for his scanning skills and efficient service.

A special debt of gratitude goes to Marc Treib, not only for contributing photographs where I needed them, but for his confidence in the success of the project, his encouragement, ruthless editing, and friendship.

Support for the project was provided by the Getty Foundation, the Graham Foundation for Advanced Studies in the Fine Arts, and the LEF Foundation. For the production I am indebted to Karen Madsen for editing; Carrie McDade for her work on the notes, bibliography, and proofing; and Miranda Hambro and Elizabeth Byrne for careful proofreading; Marc Treib for design; and naturally, our publisher William Stout for his belief in the series and his kind but relentless prodding for this volume.

In addition, I thank Robin Chandler for her unwavering belief in the value of this research and for sacrificing her weekends to see it completed.

AERIAL VIEW OF GREENWOOD COMMON, BERKELEY.

ROSE STREET IS TO THE LEFT, LE ROY BELOW, GREENWOOD TERRACE NEAR THE TOP. THE PLUM ALLÉE, UPPER RIGHT, APPEARS WITHOUT LEAVES. [CRIS BENTON, WINTER 2008]

13

Part 1:
Greenwood Common:
A Biography

Sitting between the northern California coastal range and the San Francisco Bay, Berkeley lies almost directly east of the Golden Gate, that celebrated channel separating the San Francisco peninsula from Marin County to its north. The city was named by the trustees of the College of California after George Berkeley, an eighteenth-century British philosopher and Anglican Bishop of Cloyne, Ireland.[6] What particularly attracted them was a line in one of Berkeley's poems: "Westward the course of empire takes its way."[7]

In 1867, in response to the passage of the Morrill Land Grant College Act of 1862 by the U.S. Congress, the California state legislature voted to establish a state-supported institution of higher learning.[8] The next matter to be addressed was its location. That same year, the trustees of the College of California, who were struggling financially, offered to transfer their institution and its Berkeley and Oakland properties to state control. Thus California created an instant university: courses could continue at the Oakland site while a new campus was built in Berkeley.[9] Formal transfer to state control as the University of California did not occur until 1869, and not until 1873, with the completion of North and South Halls—wood and brick confections designed squarely in the Victorian mold—did the university move to its current site [figure B-2].

In 1899, philanthropist Phoebe Apperson Hearst decided to develop the Berkeley campus into a grand educational institution to honor her late husband, Senator George Hearst, and perhaps to compete with Jane Stanford and the university she and her husband built in Palo Alto near the base of the San Francisco peninsula. Hearst chose Berkeley architect Bernard Maybeck to help her create an "Athens of the West." Maybeck was then teaching drawing in the university's engineering program, the school of architecture not yet formed.

"The International Competition for the Phoebe Hearst Architectural Plan for the University of California" was implemented in two phases. The first, held in Antwerp, was open to designers living anywhere in the world. One hundred and five entries were received before the July 1, 1898, deadline. Most proposals reflected the axial planning and classical forms then taught at the École des Beaux-Arts in Paris—and fully in accord with the competition program's vision for a monumental, classical "City of Learning." Eleven architects emerged as finalists: three from France, one each from Austria and Switzerland, and six from the eastern United States.[10]

The Antwerp victors were invited to California—at Mrs. Hearst's expense—to acquaint themselves with the realities of the site. The second judging took place in the newly completed San Francisco Ferry Building during the first week of September 1899. The winner was Émile Bénard from France. His vision was never realized, however, due to severe personality clashes with Mrs. Hearst. Hearst and Maybeck then chose the New York architect John Galen Howard who, with his partner Samuel Cauldwell, had ranked fourth in the competition. Howard began his career as the supervising architect for the University of California in 1901, and his first project was the Hearst Mining Building, a memorial to Mrs. Hearst's husband who had come to California in 1850 as a miner. In 1903, while serving as the university architect, Howard was contracted to develop the university's program in architectural education.

The town quickly grew to surround the university. Residential areas developed to the north, south, and east of the campus. To the west, three sets of tracks for railroad and streetcar lines encouraged the development of commercial and industrial areas. The City of Berkeley, which comprised nearly eleven square miles, was officially incorporated in 1878. By the beginning of 1906 its population numbered about 26,000. A year later it was 38,000, a sudden, dramatic increase due to the resettlement of refugees fleeing San Francisco in the aftermath of the earthquake and fire that destroyed a considerable part of that city.

The hills north of the campus were developed after 1903, when an electric streetcar line was built along Euclid Avenue—a line that ended at the northern entrance to the university. Euclid Avenue ran north–south on a ridge midway between the flatlands of commercial Berkeley and the crest of the hills to the east. Unlike the flat areas, which had been platted using a standard grid pattern, streets graded to the contours of the topography guided the development of the hills.

Residential architectural styles reflected the city's development, and early Berkeley residences were built in various Victorian styles. At the turn of the twentieth century, however, the more rustic Arts-and-Crafts, brown-shingle style dominated north Berkeley residential design. The style was promoted by the Berkeley Hillside Club, whose members included poet and naturalist Charles Keeler and architects Maybeck, Almeric Coxhead, John Galen Howard, and Henry Gutterson. The Club's members felt that properties should retain existing trees and use natural materials for construction.[11] In *The Simple Home* Keeler expressed

[B-2]
UNIVERSITY OF CALIFORNIA CAMPUS, BERKELEY, 1891.
[ENVIRONMENTAL DESIGN ARCHIVES, UNIVERSITY OF CALIFORNIA, HEREAFTER EDA, UCB]

his belief that houses be "rational"—simple, free of unnecessary ornament, suitable for their sites, neither pretentious nor ambitious, and of a color that blended with nature.[12] The philosophy of the group was realized primarily in the neighborhood referred to as "Northside," located in the hills to the north of the campus.

Bernard Maybeck designed numerous homes in the area including his own on Buena Vista Way. His 1913 design for the Rose Walk integrated a stepped pedestrian walkway into a planned residential community. The neighborhood was conceived by the residents as an integrated, harmonious development with Rose Walk as its central feature.[13] Although Rose Walk itself survived, the homes on it and most of the houses in the neighborhood were lost in the Berkeley fire of 1923.[14] The fire raced down the hills of Northside and destroyed five hundred residences, leaving only the handful that remain today.

The land that forms Greenwood Common was originally part of the thirty-two-acre La Loma estate owned by a nineteenth-century entrepreneur known as Captain Thomas. It was Thomas who planted the majestic Monterey pines that continue to distinguish the area. In 1903—more than a decade after Thomas's death—the prominent San Francisco attorney Warren Gregory acquired a portion of the La Loma tract including the two and a half acres of land that were to become Greenwood Common. Gregory commissioned John Galen Howard to design a country retreat for his family on this land in the Berkeley Hills.

The Warren Gregory House at 1459 Greenwood Terrace was the first in a series of houses built by the Gregorys in the area. The house is a long, two-story redwood structure with an elegant

[B-3]
JOHN GALEN HOWARD,
GREGORY RESIDENCE, BERKELEY,
1903.
PHOTOGRAPH TAKEN WHILE THE
WURSTERS RESIDED THERE.
[EDA, UCB]

living room at its south end, marked by a wall of leaded glass casement windows, a deep cross-beamed ceiling, and a large clinker-brick fireplace [figure B-3]. The house, which survived the fire of 1923, also contains a library and formal dining room. In 1906, following the San Francisco earthquake and fire, what had been a retreat became the Gregory's permanent home. The house was extended to its present size at that time. The property also included a tennis court, stable, guest house, and touch-football field.

The site falls from Greenwood Terrace on the east to Le Roy Avenue below, on its western border [figure B-4]. While living there, the Gregorys commissioned a number of houses surrounding the land that would become the Common.[15] The first house, built in 1908, was designed by Bernard Maybeck for Frances Gregory, a nurse. It is a two-and-a-half-story, wood-frame, shingled structure with an asymmetrical plan reflected in its sloped roof. The second-story bedroom projects over a deep porch supported by square timber columns that conjure associations with an East Coast colonial fort.

The house at the curve where Greenwood Terrace intersects Buena Vista Way was designed in 1913 by John Galen Howard as a commission from Warren Gregory for George Noyes, a professor of Slavic languages, who was their mutual friend. Rented for a nominal sum, it was occupied by the Noyes family until 1959. The house is a multistory, redwood-frame building in a chalet style, graced by carved balustrades that project from the south end of the house. Like both its contemporary and future neighbors, the house addresses local architectural traditions and climate, as well as a history of enclosing open rooms when additional

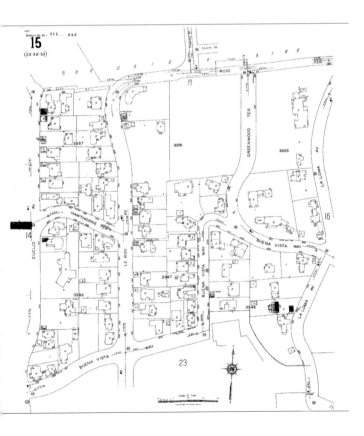

[B-4]
SANBORN FIRE INSURANCE COMPANY. MAP OF BERKELEY. ALAMEDA COUNTY, 1929-1950.
THE SITE FOR GREENWOOD COMMON IS THE OPEN SPACE AT THE TOP OF THE MAP.

interior space was required. In this case the sleeping porch balcony was glazed in the 1920s when a study adjacent to the living room was added.[16] With a similar intent, many Greenwood residents converted carports to more utilitarian garages and studies, especially in the 1960s.

At the suggestion of Warren Gregory, John Galen Howard designed his own house in 1912 on the northwestern edge of the Gregory estate, where Rose Street meets Le Roy Avenue. Designed to fit the lot, the plan takes form as a curving L-shape [figure B-5]. Although physically isolated from the Common by topography, the materials and design of this two-story brown-shingled residence harmonize with the houses that would later be built on the Common above it. In 1927 Julia Morgan added a library wing that blends so well with the original structure it is hardly noticeable as an addition.

The Vision

Warren Gregory died in 1927, but his wife Sadie lived in their Greenwood Terrace home until 1928 when she returned to live permanently in San Francisco. Elizabeth Ellis, a good friend of Sadie Gregory's, then occupied the house until her death in 1950. In 1951 William Wurster, who was then living nearby, began negotiations with Sadie Gregory and concurrently purchased an R. M. Schindler-remodeled house facing Le Roy Avenue—it would become 7 Greenwood Common—and lived there during the early stages of the sale discussions.

According to a reminiscence Wurster wrote in 1962, "The Gregorys had suggested that if I could gather a group together and present an imaginative scheme, the big lot (now the Common) would be for sale at the appraised value."[17] Wurster's decision

[B-5]

JOHN GALEN HOWARD. HOWARD RESIDENCE ["ROSE–LEROY HOUSE"], BERKELEY, 1912.

[EDA, UCB]

to purchase and develop the Gregory property was based on a number of considerations. Foremost among them were to own land in a location he loved and to design and build a home for his family. He also wanted to invest in a property that could be subdivided and developed as a community that reflected his and Catherine's philosophy of socially engaged architecture.

Initially he had planned to build a house on one of the Greenwood Common lots, but in the end he decided to keep the large Gregory house and to sell the Schindler house and adjacent land. Once the matter of his own home was settled Wurster turned his attention to developing the parcel of land that lay between it and the bay seen in the distance.

Wurster intended to encourage a group of friends and colleagues to purchase the lots to create a unique residential community. Both he and his wife, Catherine, recognized the potential of architecture to have a positive social impact on society, and that "a community defined by a group of homes could influence the way their owners lived."

The plans for Greenwood Common evolved within a complex nexus of time and relationships. For one, Wurster had a longstanding interest in the area. "In 1913," he wrote to a friend, "as a freshman I discovered Greenwood Terrace—long before I knew the Gregorys—and for a boy coming from the great Central Valley, this small street with its pine trees was sheer romance. I think I still feel the same way about it."[18] Serendipitously, he came to know the Gregorys through their son Don, who was Wurster's classmate at Berkeley. The Wursters and Gregorys became close friends following his designing, in 1927, their celebrated

summer "farmhouse" in Scotts Valley [figure B-6].[19]

Wurster had been thinking about ideal residential communities for some time and had expressed his thoughts in correspondence that responded to an article praising the Fresh Meadows development in Queens, New York, built in 1949—just a few years before his purchase of the land for Greenwood Common. Fresh Meadows was a development of 3,000 units clustered in "neighborhoods" of variously sized apartment houses designed by Voorhees, Walker, Foley & Smith for the New York Life Insurance Company. The development included carefully planned public landscapes and traffic circulation.[20] In correspondence with the architectural critic Lewis Mumford, Wurster wrote,

> I am not as enthusiastic about Fresh Meadows as you are, for none of the units have their own out-of-doors. This I feel is the greatest need of the family, the lack of which goes far toward creating the restlessness in all apartment living, particularly when it is all-year-round living.[21]

Wurster would address this issue when planning Greenwood Common—landscape and architecture received equal attention, and private gardens and open space complemented the interiors of the houses.

To determine a fair price for the Greenwood property Sadie Gregory suggested an appraisal by Frederick Duhring of the Mason-McDuffie Real Estate Company. He determined that the undeveloped parcel of land held considerable value but that the Gregory House, due to its current physical condition, had little financial worth. Wurster, concerned about insulting his friend and benefactor, asked Donald Gregory to present the appraisal to his mother. According to a 1964 interview with Wurster, she reviewed the report and said, "'Isn't

[B-6]
WILLIAM WURSTER.
WARREN GREGORY RESIDENCE,
SCOTTS VALLEY, 1924.
[ROGER STURTEVANT; EDA, UCB]

that wonderful. We'll give Bill the house.' So they literally gave me this house, and I bought the land."[22] At the time, Wurster expressed his hope to Duhring that the Gregorys would accept the proffered sum of $64,500 because that was all they could offer. He feared that if more money were needed the enterprise might fall through. He also regretted that he hadn't asked for a comprehensive appraisal rather than making distinctions between the undeveloped and developed parcels. He believed that dividing the property later might have been more beneficial financially.[23]

In 1950, following his return to California, Wurster had written to Carl Koch, his colleague at the Massachusetts Institute of Technology (MIT), requesting information about Koch's own 1940 residential development at Snake Hill in Belmont, Massachusetts.

> *I may be embarking on an enterprise to buy a piece of land to build on. There will be nine lots plus a common playground. Could you send me the legal way you did this at Smoke [sic] Hill? It would be of great help. Do all have equal schemes in the common plot or is it prorated by the size of lot—or cost of lot? If you can do this as soon as possible it will be a great convenience.[24]*

Both Snake Hill and Greenwood Common were modernist residential enclaves with individually owned plots and a corporate entity composed of the homeowners that controlled the land and roads. Both groups encouraged a similarity of exterior appearances to grant some formal homogeneity to the neighborhood. But the similarities

ended there. Although Wurster may have learned something useful about subdividing and financing from his inquiry, Snake Hill was a very different sort of development. To begin with, the project was initiated by a group of people who wanted to buy, develop, and build cooperatively. Snake Hill comprised a small number of houses sited on a rocky, wooded, and hilly piece of land along a winding road; there was only marginal terrain for the community's shared tennis courts and swimming pool [figure B-7]. The development at Six Moon Hill in Lexington, Massachusetts, also featured homes on large lots among wooded terrain [figures B-8A, B-8B]

Greenwood, in contrast, was compactly organized around a small shared green [figure B-9]. In addition, the Snake Hill houses shared a far more uniform building program that reflected Carl Koch's experience with Tech-built houses—"economic and flexible" structures using prefabricated elements and identical floor plans.[25] They demonstrated that mass-produced, standardized building parts could be put together in highly individual ways. The varying topography of building sites, however, thwarted Koch's original intentions. Instead, to retain the requisite economy they would construct five of the houses simultaneously using standard details and appliances. No such budget-driven, uniform approach to construction, design, and timing guided the realization of the houses on Greenwood Common.[26]

In his oral history, Wurster explained that he organized the group that bought Greenwood Common, subdivided the land, and made a compelling neighborhood plan so that the center lot was owned by everybody: no one could build on that site without common approval.[27] Reflecting on

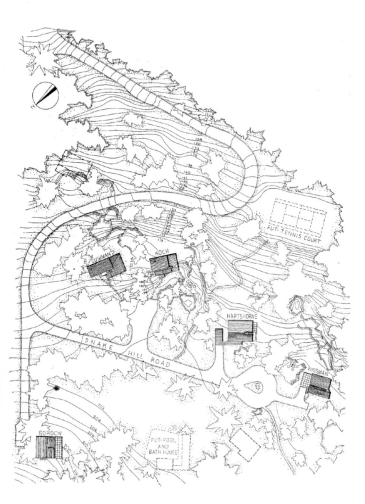

[B-7]

CARL KOCH. SNAKE HILL, BELMONT MASSACHUSETTS, 1940.

[*ARCHITECTURAL FORUM*, JUNE 1941]

[B-8A]
CARL KOCH, RESIDENCE, SNAKE
HILL, BELMONT, MASSACHUSETTS,
LATE 1940s.
[MARC TREIB]

[B-8B]
RESIDENCE, THE ARCHITECTS
COLLABORATIVE. SIX MOON HILL,
LEXINGTON, MASSACHUSETTS, 1950s.
[MARC TREIB]

the formation of the Common, the architect John Funk remembered that: "Wurster divided the land in a very special way. Instead of covering the property with individual lots, which was the standard practice of the times, he made a ring of small sites around a communally held park, reminiscent of the New England common."[28] Ultimately, "Greenwood Common, Inc.," a not-for-profit corporation, became the property's legal governing entity.

An early plan from November 1951 divided the land into ten large lots including three that bordered Greenwood Terrace. The sole entrance to the site was from an access road running along the northern lots that led to a central parking area and a wide L-shaped central lawn. From the western edge of the site, stairs descended the hill to Le Roy Avenue. Lot 10, the group's smallest, was located between the Common and the house remodeled by R. M. Schindler in which Wurster then lived.[29]

In a February 1952 memo to interested participants—Frank Newman, Harold Nachtrieb, Joseph Henry Jackson, Tom Blaisdell, and Sophus Stockholm—Wurster proposed a method for acquiring and controlling the property and included information concerning its tax status. He also listed twenty-two individuals who had expressed interest in the property and requested advice on how to reply to the inquiries.

In a reminiscence Wurster recalled that he "must have talked to 200 people to gain the 12 necessary."[30] Half of the names were connected to the university, two resided at the adjacent Rose Walk, one was employed by Kaiser Permanente, and one by Standard Oil. Interestingly, architect/professor Vernon DeMars and physicist/professor Arthur Kip were also on the list. Like Wurster, both taught at MIT following the war—Kip as a professor, DeMars as a guest lecturer—before coming to Berkeley.[31] Buckminster Fuller was initially included in the list of possible participants in Greenwood's development but replied to Wurster's invitation by saying that as much as he would have loved to make such a move, he was unable to do so for financial reasons.[32] Wurster responded that "it would have been a deep joy" to have had him live on Greenwood Common.

The early plan raised issues about costs, access for people and cars, private space, public areas, and views. In response, Wurster's succeeding design of March 1952 included twelve smaller lots—three of them located along Greenwood Terrace—as well as the central common and stairs leading down to Le Roy Avenue [figure B-10]. The new plan, reflecting more closely the final division of the site, provided access from Greenwood Terrace at three points, retaining the original idea of a main vehicle access leading to an internal parking area—albeit reduced in size—and a secondary road to the south. The third point of access was a pedestrian walk to common land at the site's center. Wurster explained the modifications in an accompanying memo, noting that reducing the lot sizes to 5,000 square feet not only lowered the cost per lot but also gave owners a larger common space. And he explained that as "one lives with the property" one recognizes the need to open a vista of the Common from Greenwood Terrace to provide a view from the street and a dramatic entrance for all.[33]

Once the final site plan was determined things began moving rapidly. Sadie Gregory wrote to Wurster on April 18 bestowing her "blessings on

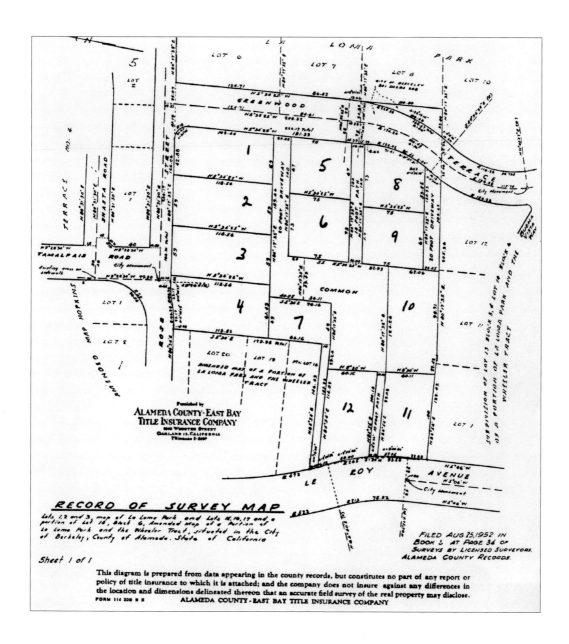

RECORD OF SURVEY MAP

[B-9]

GREENWOOD COMMON, SURVEY
MAP, 25 AUGUST 1952.

NORTH IS TO THE LEFT.
[COURTESY GREENWOOD COMMON,
INC., BOARD OF DIRECTORS]

Greenwood Common and its occupants." In an April 24, 1952, memo to participants, Wurster stated that while it was "best not to become entangled in restrictions, certain things have been mentioned which might be listed in order to have a harmonious project with minimum disappointments or friction."[34] By this time three of the south side lots appear to have been sold or at least claimed by individuals who eventually built there. These were lot 8 (Douglas), lot 9 (Blaisdell), and lot 10 (Maenchen).

All the owners received a list of ten topics prior to their May meeting, where free and open discussion was to be encouraged. Among the topics for discussion were the height of television antennae, the types and number of trees, the shape of roofs, steps to Le Roy Avenue, the adoption of uniform fencing, and the approximate character of the plot plan. Also slated for discussion was a suggestion that the houses on the flat areas rise no higher than a single story so that the Common would appear more spacious, as well as the idea that dark-colored houses (either natural woods or paint) would also contribute to a feeling of spaciousness. Wurster also suggested that if the Rose Street houses (lots 1, 2, 3, and 4) were kept to the north ends of their lots, each could have a sheltered south garden that would add to the unity of the project.[35] This was a strategy Wurster had used in several San Francisco townhouses, most notably his Grover house of 1939.

In the end, privacy for each home won out over open gardens, and each lot came to have a fence at its south edge that separated it from the Common. Although perhaps not Wurster's intended concept, the fences do serve as a common unifying architectural element. The residents' developing

guidelines for the visual relationships of the designs and materials could be read as a precedent for the development of The Sea Ranch on the Sonoma Coast a decade later—although there the guidelines were determined by the architects and developer.

The entity known as Greenwood Common, Inc., filed articles of incorporation with the State of California on June 29, 1952 [see figure B-9]. Incorporated as a recreational organization, the purposes of the corporation were social and included owning and managing property, both real and personal, and conducting activities intended to benefit the owners and occupants of Greenwood Common Properties. The corporation would also exercise rights and powers granted to nonprofit organizations and would not be authorized to issue stock or to distribute profits or dividends to its members except upon dissolution.[36] According to the articles, the members of the corporation were the owners of lots in Greenwood Common Properties, and were, in accordance with the by-laws, to elect directors and "take actions" at their annual meeting.

Following registration, the Board of Directors adopted the official survey map of August 1952 as a section of the by-laws and defined the final arrangement and number of the constituent properties. Each member of the corporation was to deposit the purchase price of their lot with the title company, after which it would act as trustee to purchase the entire property from Mrs. Gregory, thereafter deeding the individual lots to the specific members. The total property—twelve lots and the Common—was purchased in 1952 for approximately $67,000. Each member purchased one or more of the twelve lots with no separate value set on the shared open space.

The first directors—all owners or intended owners—of Greenwood Common lots were Robert Birge, Frederick Duhring, Charlotte Morrison, Sophus Stockholm, and William W. Wurster. Birge and Duhring became residents of the Common, and Wurster (who had intended to design a house for his family) ended up living across the street in the Gregory House until his death in 1973. Morrison does not appear to have continued her relationship with Greenwood Common; Stockholm did not build on his lot and later sold it. However, Stockholm, a builder, continued a professional relationship with Wurster and his firm, as indicated by correspondence found in the Wurster Bernardi & Emmons archives.

The Common was now officially established and its lots numbered; ten owners had committed.

Each of the twelve lots had a veto right on the sale or development of the common areas, and the by-laws provided that any action affecting land held by the Corporation or members' rights of access to their lots required approval of all twelve members.[37] The deed for each of the twelve lots was encumbered with an obligation to contribute to the maintenance costs of the public spaces as a whole.

Because lots 11 and 12 were located on the steep slope west of the flat portion of the Common, they were held to height restrictions that insured any construction would not disturb the view from the common area above. They were given right of access to the Common using stairs to be built on a ten-foot-wide easement on commonly held land.[38]

The first meeting of the board was called for July 22, 1952, at the Wursters' home. Business included adopting the by-laws, appointing officers (chairman and secretary), and finding a replacement for Charlotte Morrison. By September, title to the Greenwood Property had been transferred from Sadie Gregory to Greenwood Common, Inc., and the list of owners confirmed.

The Samuel Schaafs were now the proud owners of lot 2 and the Walter Olivers purchased lot 12. Wurster served as the first chairman of the Board. The process of subdividing and developing Greenwood Common served as a successful example of building quality homes on a small parcel of land while providing a sense of suburban space [figure B-11].[39]

The shapes and locations of the lots as well as issues of slope, views, privacy, and parking directed the house designs. The residences built on the flat south side of the Common were kept to a single story, with carports positioned to the sides or rear, and windows and gardens oriented to the Common or bay. In contrast, structures built on the north side profited from their downward-sloping lots by incorporating lower floors facing Rose Street. In addition to access to the half-acre Common, each family would also have a garden of its own.

Members of the academic community purchased their lots because of their proximity to campus, the opportunity to participate in an innovative living situation, and their desire to build new homes. The result was a homogeneous neighborhood of white, upper-middle-class, liberal, professional, well-educated individuals and families. Drs. Robert and Anne Birge, owners of lot 1, were respectively, associate director of the physics division of the Berkeley Radiation Laboratory and professor of physics at California State University at Hayward.

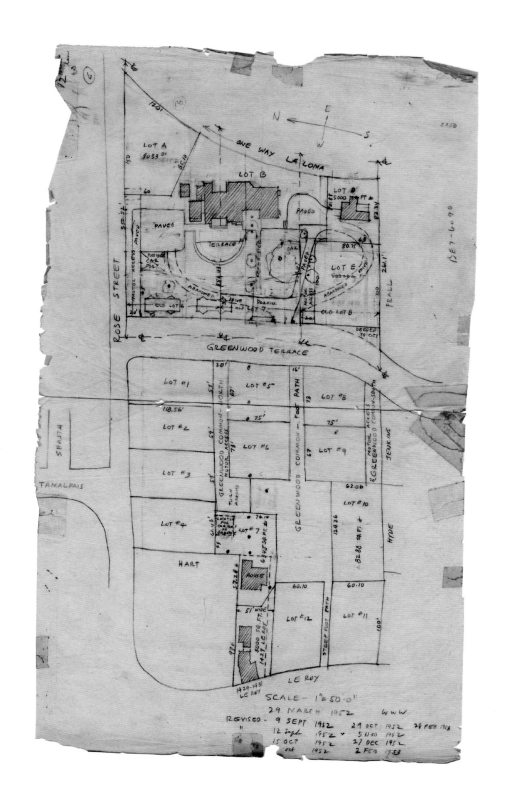

SCALE — 1"=50·0'

29 MARCH 1952   W W W

REVISED - 9 SEPT 1952   29 OCT 1952   24 FEB 1953
    "   12 Sept 1952 *   5 Nov 1952
    "   15 OCT 1952   27 DEC 1952
    "   oct 1952   2 FEB 1953

28

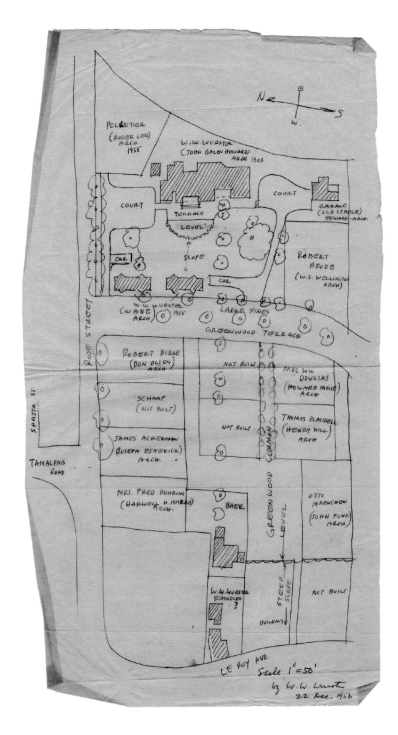

N
E
S
W

PELLETIER
(ROGER LEE
ARCH
1955

W.W. WURSTER
(JOHN GALEN HOWARD)
ARCH. 1903

COURT

COURT

GARAGE
(OLD STABLE)
HOWARD ARCH.

TERRACE
LEVEL

ROBERT
BRODE
(W.S. WELLINGTON
ARCH)

CAR

SLOPE

ROSE STREET

CAR

W.W. WURSTER
(WB&E
ARCH)
1955

LARGE PINES

GREENWOOD TERRACE

ROBERT BIRGE
(DON OLSEN
ARCH)

NOT BUILT

MRS WW
DOUGLAS
(HOWARD MOISE)
ARCH

S. SHASTA ST.

SCHAAP
(NOT BUILT)

NOT BUILT

THOMAS BLAISDELL
(HENRY HILL
ARCH)

JAMES ACKERMAN
(JOSEPH ESHERICK)
ARCH

GREENWOOD COMMON

TANALPAIS
ROAD

MRS. FRED DUHRING
(HARWELL H. HARRIS)
ARCH

BAER

OTTO
MAENCHEN
(JOHN FUNK
ARCH)

GREENWOOD LEVEL

W.W. WURSTER
SCHINDLER
?

STEEP SLOPE

NOT BUILT

BUILDING

LE ROY AVE

Scale 1" = 50'

by W.W. Wurster
22 Dec. 1956

[B-10] *opposite*

**WILLIAM WURSTER, GREENWOOD
COMMON, SITE PLAN, 1953.**

SHADING INDICATES PROPERTIES
OWNED BY WURSTER.
[COURTESY SADIE SUPER]

[B-11] *above*

**WILLIAM WURSTER, GREENWOOD
COMMON, SITE PLAN, 1956.**

NOTE WURSTER'S RECONFIGURATION
OF LOT 7 AND THE OWNER'S NAME
ON EACH PROPERTY.
[COURTESY SADIE SUPER]

According to Ann Birge, they spent an hour with Wurster absorbing his concept of the Common and how he envisioned lot owners would develop their properties.[40]

Lot 2 was initially purchased by astrophysicist Alexander Bratenahl, who had expected to remain in Berkeley upon completion of his dissertation in 1952. When he instead joined the Jet Propulsion Lab at the California Institute of Technology in southern California, he sold his property to Samuel Schaaf, professor of mechanical engineering at the university. James Ackerman, art historian and the first professor of architectural history on the Berkeley campus, purchased lot 3 from Frederick Duhring to build a one-story house for his wife after she contracted polio and could no longer manage living in their multi-level home. The Frederick Duhrings, who had also purchased lot 4, were not affiliated with the university; Mr. Duhring was an agent with the real estate firm Mason McDuffie and had assisted Wurster with the appraisal and purchase of the original property.

Lots 5 and 6, located on the west side of Greenwood Terrace, were purchased by Sophus Stockholm and David Russell, respectively, but never developed. It is likely that Russell, who then purchased lot 5 in the early 1960s, had fully intended to develop the lots and why he didn't is not known. Whatever the reason, Russell's decision was fortuitous as both lots were maintained as open space and over time came to be considered part of the common areas. The Russell heirs, who resided on the East Coast, maintained their option for building on lots 5 and 6. But after 25 years of not exercising that option, in 1976 they offered to sell their holdings to the residents of the Common at their appraised value. Not building on these two lots maintained the unobstructed view from Greenwood Terrace to the west and preserved the openness of the common. In 1977 the owners of the eight houses on the Common agreed to purchase the two lots and add them to the commonly held open space. Not developing the two lots contributed enormously to the identity of the Common, both for the residents and the wider community. Rather than simply a closed community with a common space at its center, Greenwood Common became the epitome of modern Californian indoor-outdoor living—an open green area with a stupendous view of the San Francisco Bay shared by the owners of its homes and their neighbors.

The lot owned by Wurster was divided into halves, with his residence incorporated into lot 7 and oriented to face the Common. The remaining half of the property would be sold separately and oriented toward Le Roy Avenue. To enhance the meager dimensions of lot 7 Wurster added the part of his adjacent parcel that abutted lot 7, separating it from the part that sloped down to Le Roy Avenue. A 1920s house that R. M. Schindler had remodeled for Sasha Kaun in 1940 already stood on this new, larger lot 7; Wurster and his family had briefly lived there and remodeled parts of the house. Wurster sold the property to his colleague, architectural photographer Morley Baer, following his move into the Gregory house in 1952. Baer worked with the architect Henry Hill to expand the spaces of the house.

Lot 8 was owned by Helen Douglas, a widow who, at the time of Greenwood Common's establishment in 1952, lived nearby. She required a small house with a sunny garden and hired Howard Moïse, professor of architecture at the University of California, Berkeley, to be her architect. Clients for the house on lot 9, designed by Henry Hill, were Thomas C. and Catherine Maltby Blaisdell, also then living in the neighborhood. Dr. Blaisdell served as Assistant Secretary of Commerce under President Harry Truman and joined the Berkeley faculty as professor of political science in 1951. Mrs. Blaisdell was an educator and active in a variety of civic organizations. John Funk designed the house on lot 10 for Otto and Anna Maenchen. Both were Viennese and taught at the university: he in art history; she in psychiatry.

In time it became clear that lots 11 and 12 were too steep to be successfully integrated into the upper part of the Common although the owners of these lots were still considered equal members of the Corporation with full voting rights. After building their own house, the Maenchens purchased lot 11 below it, both as an investment and to preserve their tranquility and view. With John Funk they planned a small house for the site but it was never realized and the lot was later sold. Physically removed from both the topography and community of Greenwood Common, the residences ultimately constructed on lots 11 and 12 were given addresses on Le Roy Avenue.[41]

The site design of the Common was carefully configured to provide privacy for every house and to provide three points of entry.[42] Vehicles used a paved access road from Greenwood Terrace to residential carports and a small shared parking area. Pedestrians could enter from the east under a formal allée of flowering plum trees or by using stairs from Le Roy Avenue on the original easement assigned to access the homes on lots 11 and 12. When it became evident that those two lots were too steep to develop, the stair's maintenance was relaxed. Remnants of these stairs exist, but no access today links Le Roy Avenue to the Common.

Vision Becomes Reality

All the residences on the Common reflect a symbiotic relationship between modernism and local tradition, and between indoor and outdoor spaces. Most of the architects who worked there practiced an aesthetic that reflected the desire for a uniquely California lifestyle that engaged the mild climate, the geography, and the environment, using wood as their preferred building material. Each residence serves as an example of the postwar house described by Gardner Dailey in his brief essay for the San Francisco Museum of Art's 1949 exhibition "Domestic Architecture of the San Francisco Bay Region." In it, Dailey describes the postwar home as the "Large-Small House," centering on one very large room with the balance of the house compressed to eliminate wasted space—such as long halls, stairs, and basements—reducing services, and replacing the enclosed garage with a simple roof.[43] Dailey's description of the residences featured in the exhibition applies aptly to those on the Common:

> Almost all of the houses shown use what had become popularly known as the dual-purpose room. By this we mean the Playroom-Garden Room, the Study-Guest Room, the Living Dining-Room, the Dining-Kitchen Room; the Pantry has become only a vestige and it is only man's basic instinct to worship fire, which still keeps the fireplace intact in the Living Room. Storage space on the other hand, has been greatly increased as this Age has become a collector of equipment, clothes, and gadgets. Wherever possible, things are "built-in" and integrated with the house.[44]

The plan of Greenwood Common, simply speaking, comprises two flanks of residences that run east-west: on the north flank are the lots numbered 1 to 4; on the south, those numbered 8 to 10. The remodeled Schindler house on lot 7 terminates the north flank on the bay side. The south side of the enclave was developed first. The Blaisdells (lot 9) and Maenchens (lot 10) began construction almost immediately. Early in February 1953 the property owners and their architects, Henry Hill and John Funk, received information from the Berkeley authorities concerning the development of the project's infrastructure: concerns such as paving, path width, the number and placement of power poles, and the locations of water, sewer, and gas lines. To provide automobile access a twenty-foot-wide driveway terminated by parking spaces for three cars fronted the lots on the north side of the Common. A driveway on the south edge of the property behind lots 8 and 9, ending in the garage of the Maenchen house on lot 10, provided automobile access for the south flank of houses.

Thomas Blaisdell was selected as chairman at the annual meeting of the members of Greenwood Common, Inc. in September of 1953. It was at this meeting that the plans for the landscape and paving were addressed, "especially in view of the early completion of the Maenchen house."[45] Later that fall the members failed to locate the address of Stockholm's successor and also raised concerns about the stepping stones the Maenchens were placing on common property. The Maenchens responded that they were necessary for the safety of delivery people.

William Wurster developed the Greenwood Common site as an ideal environment for himself and his family. As a developer-resident, he wanted to build a social community of interesting, creative, and educated individuals. As an architect and architectural educator, he wanted this small residential community to demonstrate the highest standards of housing and garden design in California.

As house construction began, Wurster personally engaged with both the residents and their architects, and despite not being a member of the Common, he maintained a strong interest—both personally and professionally—in its construction. This involvement is clearly reflected in his correspondence throughout the period. For example, in one letter he expressed his curiosity to Harwell Hamilton Harris about his designs for the Duhring residence, and in another wrote to a friend in New York that "Helen Douglas has a delightful place—both house and garden—and we see her frequently."[46]

Wurster maintained an ambivalent role in the Common's architectural development. He took an active interest in the design of the houses but tried not to dictate his tastes or ideas. The Birges recalled that after that initial discussion Wurster did not interfere in the relations between the clients and their architects. Esherick concurred with Wurster's lack of design review, recalling that "Bill did not try to impose his ideas to the extent of looking over the drawings and saying Yeah, that's okay, but don't do this."[47]

"There wasn't much of a housing shortage at the time," noted James Ackerman. "I think Bill Wurster, who had been asked by the Gregory heirs to do the subdivision, didn't believe that it was proper for him to design one of the houses;

and, as you say, he was interested in promoting others, even his contemporary Howard Moïse."[48] Joseph Esherick, who designed the Ackerman house, remembered the development of Greenwood Common as a kind of academic exercise that seemed an almost unnatural, esoteric idea of an idealized little community.[49]

To Wurster—who had a professional relationship with most of the architects who designed homes for the Common—the project must have seemed a natural extension of his professional and academic lives. Both Donald Olsen and John Funk had worked in his office, and Howard Moïse and Joseph Esherick were members of the architecture faculty at Berkeley. He had known Harwell Hamilton Harris professionally since the 1930s and Henry Hill through Bay Area professional circles.

In a long letter to property owner Bob Birge, Wurster noted that although he was "touched and pleased" to be invited to the board meeting held in October, he demurred on the grounds that it would "be simpler all around if your meeting has only those who are part of the Common." He added that he was happy with the houses built to date and looked forward to the completion of Birge's own home.[50] Wurster's association with the project had both good and bad moments. In a 1954 letter to his friend Texas architect O'Neil Ford, he explained that although he had given a year of his life to the Greenwood Common venture, he "refused to design any houses for it as it was too close to home." The letter displayed both Wurster's discomfort with a disagreement with Harwell Harris about his design and his pleasure that Howard Moïse and Henry Hill had courteously shown him their plans and solicited his advice; John Funk also reviewed his design with Wurster.[51]

That all the residents were grateful to Wurster for his role in the development of the Common is perhaps best summarized by this 1953 letter from Catherine Blaisdell.

Dear Bill,

This note is inevitable as night follows day Saying "Thank you" sounds inadequate, writing it even less so—but Tom and I do want you to know how very much we appreciate all you and Catherine did to make it possible for Tom and me to have this unbelievably beautiful spot for our new home in Berkeley. Neither one of us can really believe it is us—who are here. We sit and look at the stars and the lights in the evening. We gasp as we look up at the pines. Literally—we are speechless. I go round and round in sort of a daze.

All we can hope is that you two and your bewitching Sadie will be as happy in your dream house as we are in ours.

If you ever need a cup of sugar or those things called dollars. Try us, we'll always do our best!

Affectionately Yours,
Catherine Blaisdell

April 15, 1953
9 Greenwood Common[52]

Although at first glance it might appear that the property owners may have shared a common philosophy, accomplishing things was not always easy. James Ackerman, a member of the landscape committee, working with the landscape contractor Tak Sakahashi—who was implementing Halprin's design—wrote, "I am unusually loaded at the university and haven't been able to spur the plans on their round of the common members but just tonight gave a big push and hope to set something in motion. I wish I were doing this alone, but in this little stronghold of individualism one needs some patient fortitude."[53]

Once the lots were sold and homes were under construction, Wurster began to develop the remainder of his property. To offset his tax burden, as early as 1954 he considered building two small brown-shingled garden houses on 5,000-square-foot lots across the street from the Common. He envisioned them as "really small," containing a living room with kitchen alcove, bath, and bedroom.[54] In 1955 he informed his architect friend Robert Woods Kennedy in Massachusetts that he would be building two little houses of his own to rent: "Funny little things in which I aim at a sympathy with our own shingles rather than with the gravel roofs across the street."[55] That year, construction at 1429 Greenwood Terrace and 1439 Greenwood Terrace—designed by Wurster Bernardi & Emmons as four-room single-family rental units—was realized.

Also in 1955, an eager Wurster wrote to Donald Gregory about the possible purchase of Mrs. Gregory's garage lot on Greenwood Terrace, a purchase that would both round out his holdings of the Gregory property and provide him with yet another rental unit. This purchase completed, Wurster constructed a new garage with living space above it. Designed with an exterior of Douglas fir to blend into the surroundings, 1409 Greenwood Terrace, to the north of his residence, was completed in 1960 [figure B-12].[56]

The availability of land and the excitement about Wurster's proposed community generated interest in local residential buildings in a similar regional modernist vocabulary.

For example, in 1955 architect Roger Lee designed a residence for Joseph Pelletier northeast of Wurster's house, with a short walk from Greenwood Terrace [figure B-13]. Warren Callister designed the Japanese-influenced Flowers House on Rose Street across from Greenwood Terrace. At the same time physics professor R. B. Brode commissioned a residence across from 8 Greenwood Common. Designed by architect and design professor Winfield Scott Wellington, this house has two wings—built in two stages—sheathed with redwood siding and detailed with vertical lines of exposed nails that match those of the Douglas house across the street.[57]

As a corporation, Greenwood Common, Inc. elected officers, held annual meetings, and formed committees. Many issues were actively discussed but not all were acted on. Demands on the residents continued even though their homes and gardens, as well as the landscape of the Common, were completed by the close of the 1950s. The minutes of the annual Board of Directors' meetings for the 1960s reveal discussions centered primarily on practical matters such as establishing the annual assessment, placing lights on the Common, paving Greenwood Terrace (a cost shared by Wurster and Brode, who lived across the street), and whether it was worth a hundred dollars to purchase a flagpole (it wasn't). Landscape committees came and went throughout the decade and handled such matters as hiring a gardener when it became clear that cutting, watering, and mowing the lawn had become too onerous for the members themselves.[58]

[B-12]
WURSTER, BERNARDI & EMMONS,
1409 GREENWOOD TERRACE,
BERKELEY, 1960.
NORTH AND SOUTH ELEVATIONS.
[EDA, UCB]

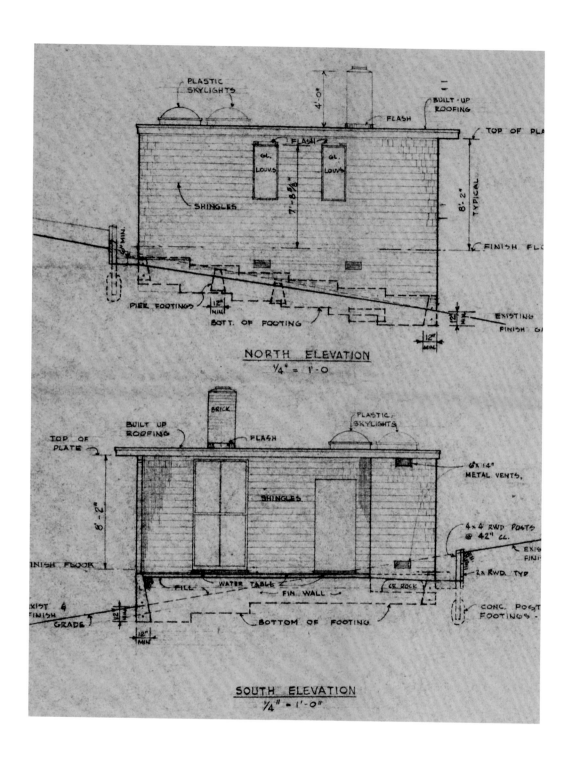

PLASTIC SKYLIGHTS

BUILT-UP ROOFING

FLASH

4'-0"

TOP OF PLA

FLASH

GL. LOUVS

GL. LOUVS

7'-8⅝"

8'-2" TYPICAL

FINISH FLO

SHINGLES

PIER FOOTINGS

12" MIN

BOTT. OF FOOTING

12" MIN

EXISTING FINISH G

12" MIN.

NORTH ELEVATION
¼" = 1'-0

BRICK

BUILT UP ROOFING

FLASH

PLASTIC SKYLIGHTS

TOP OF PLATE

8'-2"

SHINGLES

6"x 14" METAL VENTS,

4 x 4 RWD POSTS @ 42" CC.

FINISH FLOOR

EXIS FINI

2 x RWD. TYP

EXIST & FINISH GRADE

1½" MIN

12" MIN

FILL

WATER TABLE

FIN. WALL

CR. ROCK

CONC. POST FOOTINGS

BOTTOM OF FOOTING

SOUTH ELEVATION
¼" = 1'-0"

The Common was not immune to the fears of the Cold War. Perhaps because some of its residents were physicists, or simply because it was a frequent concern at the time, the Board of Directors investigated the possibility of a fallout shelter that might be used collectively by all the families. They met with an Admiral Cook of the U.S. Office of Civil Defense who informed them that simple plans for group shelters were available for their use. In the end, however, for economic more than social reasons, they decided that the matter of shelter should be considered an individual rather than a group problem.

Other areas of concern included safety and limiting access to the Common. The Board felt that signs reading "Private Road" and "Private Walk" would be more effective than a small chain or gate at the east end of the site. In the end they decided on a gate to discourage "bicyclists, children, sun bathers, and perhaps even dogs." The matter of security centered on increased lighting and an alarm system. They agreed, however, that the most cost-effective solution to provide some protection would be if all residents would keep their porch lights burning all night.[59]

By 1975 the members had recognized that the Common would be significantly enhanced by purchasing the central, and still unbuilt, Russell lots to expand the shared open space. The Board of Directors delegated a committee to contact the Russell trustees to secure the right of first refusal should the lots be put up for sale. The committee determined that their options were to purchase a portion of lot 6—thereby reducing the area to a site suitable for only a single house —or the outright purchase of both lots. Two years later Greenwood Common, Inc., purchased lots 5 and 6, combining their area with the existing common space. This land purchase necessitated the creation of new by-laws to replace those of 1952. The modifications reduced the number of full-partner shares from twelve to ten, thereby providing each owner with a ten percent share in the assets of the corporation. In addition, because the owners of lots 11 and 12 facing Le Roy Avenue were not sharing the acquisition costs of the central lots, they would no longer have voting rights on issues concerning the common open space. This arrangement permanently limited the annual assessment for lots 11 and 12 to sixty percent of the amount contributed by the other members.

Early photographs taken of the northside houses show them with gardens open to the Common. Ironically, within the first few years—sometime after the Schaaf house was completed in 1957— the gardens of houses 1 through 4 and 7 were enclosed by fences. It is unclear whether the intention behind the building of these fences was to insure privacy from common spaces or from the anticipated proximity of homes being built on lots 5 and 6. Had the residents known that these lots would remain open, they might have chosen garden designs that more directly engaged the Common.

Looking back years after he had left his house on Greenwood Common, the photographer Morley Baer remarked that it was Wurster's idea of the community, his suggestion of younger architects for various houses, and his somewhat removed but nevertheless substantial interest in the Common that made it possible for a number of very individualistic families to live together in harmony—and to do so without the usual written laws, rules, and limitations.[60] Unfortunately, the changing times, the changes of ownership, or some combination of both, affected the structure and operation of the community—changes revealed by the increasing legal and bureaucratic issues addressed by the members of the Board of Directors during the last decades of the twentieth century.

The first of these concerns was the need to add personal injury to the group insurance coverage and to add the words "private property" to the street signs as protection against liability claims. Another matter concerned the composition of the Board of Directors itself. Initially members served one-year terms, a period extended to two- and three-year terms early on. Nevertheless, the pool from which to select board members was extremely limited. Originally, after a property had been represented on the board, an absence of a full year was required before its representation could be renewed. To ameliorate this situation the definition of "member" was changed from "lot owner" to "individual resident," allowing a second owner to succeed the term of his or her spouse. While providing a larger pool, the modification proscribed owners of the same lot from serving simultaneously on the Board; there remained one vote per lot.

Members of the Common were also forced to address a particularly troublesome issue, that of maintaining the Common as a confederation of single-family residences. The concern arose in response to Mrs. Maenchen's intent to rent the living unit in her basement. The members of the Common were adamant in their desire to keep the Common from being rezoned for additional residences or to have the Maenchen unit grandfathered as an unwelcome precedent. The dispute was unpleasant and continued for much of the

1970s, resulting in a signed declaration retaining the single-family dwelling status stipulated in the by-laws, but Maenchen's need for live-in help within the primary living unit was recognized as being distinct from a renter in a second unit.

In the late 1980s a developer purchased lot 9 with the intention of adding a second story to the house. This issue stirred dissension among the residents and led to considerable rancor. The members opposed to the change claimed that it would exert a negative impact on the Common in very significant ways. Not only would the increased height distort Hill's original design, but the greater volume would cast more of the Common into shade, affect the survival of the plum trees, block views from the homes on the north side, and change the Common's "entire nature and architectural integrity."[61] Residents and their heirs in favor of the addition argued for the individual homeowner's right to make changes to his or her property. The records created during this controversy make an interesting distinction between the Common (the eight lots facing the shared space) and the Corporation (all ten lots including the two on Le Roy Avenue). For financial reasons, this distinction had been determined during the acquisition of the undeveloped central lots but had been enunciated explicitly for "political" reasons, i.e., so that only the eight lots (not all ten lots) had a say in what took place within the Common and its buildings.

In response to the proposed remodeling and despite reservations, Common homeowners applied to the Berkeley Landmarks Preservation Commission in December 1989 for landmark status. In an August 1989 letter in support of the application, Lawrence Halprin wrote:

The Greenwood Common project was a unique and avant garde project for its time. There was a wonderful collaboration of landscape and architecture. It was evidenced by the congruence of the modest, elegant architecture which was all of a Bay Area Modern Style—all in scale and built around a common area.[62]

In 1990 landmark status was granted, and the developer sold the home to its current resident. According to the conditions of the landmark listing, owners may alter the interior of a home but are required to maintain the historic design on its exterior.

Wurster's vision yielded a successful designed community that is still admired more than half a century later. In a letter to the Berkeley Landmarks Preservation Committee in 1990, James Ackerman, one of the first group of residents, recalled:

It was Wurster's intention, conveyed to prospective purchasers, that the houses on the Common would constitute a kind of architectural museum of work in what was called "The Bay Region Style," an important regional manifestation of contemporary architecture. As a result several of the most distinguished architects of the area were commissioned to do the houses there, and the Common became a showplace. Architects and scholars from elsewhere, many from Europe, made a point to visit the Common because of its reputation as one of the small number of modern design complexes in the area at the time.[63]

At Greenwood Common, a group of upper-middle-class professionals, working with established architects and landscape architects, created homes for themselves in a park setting. This small cluster of residences surrounding a shared open space combined a sense of the suburbs with the intimacy of a small town—all nestled in the Berkeley Hills in close proximity to the university that employed most of them. As a result Greenwood Common has become an icon of regional midcentury modernism and continues to thrive as a well-maintained and comfortable community site—all as it was originally intended.

[B-13]
ROGER LEE, PELLETIER RESIDENCE,
GREENWOOD TERRACE, BERKELEY,
1956.
[EDA, UCB]

RESIDENCE for MR. & MRS. JOSEPH PELLETIER

GREENWOOD COMMON, BERKELEY CALIFORNIA

ROGER LEE
ARCHITECT
2576 SHATTUCK AVENUE
BERKELEY 4, CALIFORNIA

3-7-55

39

Part 2:
The Landscape of Greenwood Common

Ten years before there was The Sea Ranch, there was Greenwood Common. Lawrence Halprin was responsible for the overall landscape planning and design for both projects. According to Halprin, at the time Wurster was first developing the site in 1952, he requested Halprin's advice on trees to be planted on either side of the sole pedestrian path into the Common. Halprin recommended flowering plums and set their spacing to establish the shared open areas, reflecting that "if I didn't do something to define the path as an entrance, the Common would get lost."[64] Three years later, Halprin was hired to prepare a comprehensive landscape plan for the Common.

Lawrence Halprin (b. 1916) was raised in New York. Following graduation from high school he spent three years in Palestine on a kibbutz, an experience he credits with confirming his utopian ideals. After returning to the United States he attended Cornell University, graduated with a degree in plant sciences, and subsequently pursued a Ph.D. in botany at the University of Wisconsin. It was in Wisconsin that he discovered his affinity for both architecture and landscape design. While researching these professions in the university library he found Christopher Tunnard's *Gardens in the Modern Landscape* (1938). Shortly thereafter he decided on landscape architecture and began taking the university's limited offerings. It was clear that Wisconsin offered insufficient opportunity for Halprin to pursue his interests so he continued his education at Harvard University.[65]

While at Harvard in the 1940s he and William Wurster developed a friendship. One summer they spent part of their vacation bicycling together through Cape Cod. During World War II Halprin served as a Lieutenant, j.g. in the Navy. His ship

[L-1]
PLUM ALLÉE IN BLOOM.
[CRIS BENTON, 2008]

41

was damaged during a kamikaze attack; he was sent to San Francisco for recovery, and there he remained after his discharge from service. Soon after arriving in the Bay Area he telephoned Wurster to see if he knew of any available professional positions. Wurster told Halprin to contact his firm.

However, once he arrived there he was told that the noted landscape architect Thomas Church "has dibs on you first as a landscape architect." It was clear that either Wurster or someone else in his office had spoken to Church, Wurster's close friend and colleague. Although Halprin loved architecture, he felt he had a better feeling for landscape.[66]

It was only natural for Wurster to have Halprin design a small garden for his new home on Greenwood Terrace in 1953. During this time Wurster discussed his ideas for Greenwood Common with Halprin, which resulted in an April 1953 memo from Wurster to the "participants in Greenwood Common" relaying Halprin's suggestions for planting Thundercloud purple plums (*Prunus cerasifera* 'Thundercloud'), removing two cypress trees and covering six feet on each side of the path with gravel.[67] According to the Board meetings of that May, the center path and two roadways had been constructed and the decision made to purchase the plum trees, which were planted later that year.[68]

By 1955, with the exception of lots 2, 5, and 6, the residences on the Common were completed or nearly so [figures L-2, L-3]. The residents then turned their collective attention to improving the landscape. According to Halprin's January 1955 letter to Morley Baer, his original suggestions included the plum allée and other details.[69] A 1953 Halprin drawing for the Maenchens pictured the newly planted allée and a rectangular central area, with proposed additional plums extending north past the Baer residence and terminating at the Duhring house [figure L-4]. This row of trees defined a north-south axis with the assumption that lots 5 and 6 would be built on. The second row of plums was never planted, the homes for the center lots never constructed.

Halprin also recommended that a committee be formed to devise a landscape program that would address use, cost, maintenance requirements, stages of development, and the "quality they would like to have; collect survey information; and interview landscape architects."[70] Following Halprin's advice a landscape committee, comprised of Morley Baer, James Ackerman, and Ann Birge, interviewed the landscape architects Geraldine Knight Scott and Robert Tetlow prior to engaging Halprin for the design work.

In their June 1955 meeting with Geraldine Knight Scott about plans for the grounds they discussed tree planting, groundcovers, irrigation systems, types of pines, parking, and special funding. Scott favored "planting trees heavily in spots, lightly elsewhere, and leaving open spaces for recreation." She was concerned about the age and longevity of the existing pines, preferred Bishop over Monterey pines, and suggested the use of grass rather than tanbark or pebbles because it was the cheapest to install, although not to maintain.[71]

A report dated the same month documented a discussion between Halprin and the landscape committee. Halprin thought the common area should function as a community center rather than as a decorative piece and favored leaving it open and simple; like Scott, he proposed using grass as the principal groundcover [figure L-5].

[L-2] *opposite above*
LAWRENCE HALPRIN (ATTRIBUTED),
SKETCH SITE PLAN, NO DATE.
THE DRAWING SHOWS THE HOUSES, EXISTING VEGETATION, PLUM ALLEE AND ROW OF PEACH TREES.
[EDA, UCB]

[L-3] *opposite below*
GREENWOOD COMMON PRIOR TO
LANDSCAPE IMPROVEMENTS.
VIEW FROM WEST, c. 1954.
[MORLEY BAER, UCSC]

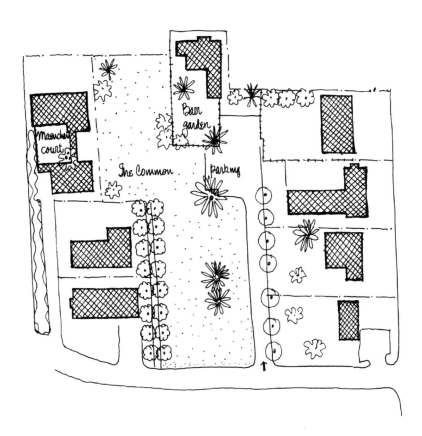

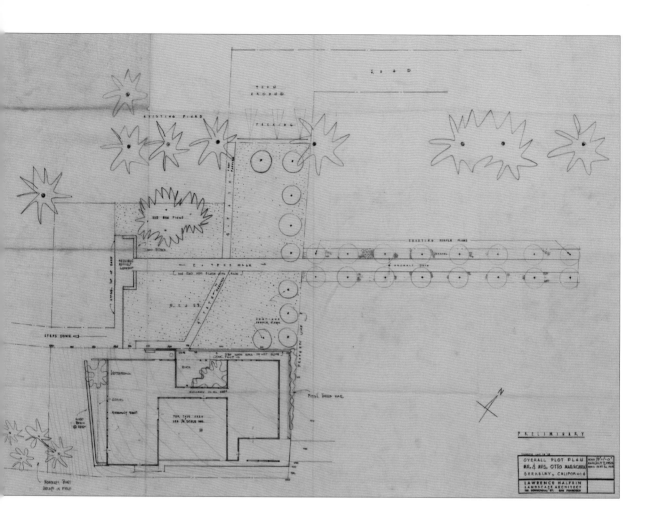

44

Grass, he felt, would allow the area to be used for a variety of activities with reasonable maintenance costs. Contrary to Scott, he preferred a large open area with plantings relegated to the periphery; a minimum of trees would supplement the gardens and play areas of the individual lots. More specifically, Halprin felt that the last two plum trees, like the existing path to the Maenchen house, should be moved because they "cut up the area badly."[72] That Halprin envisioned an integration of the shared open space with the individual lots implies that the individual property fences were not yet in place.

In August that year, the same group met with Robert Tetlow. Both Scott and Tetlow taught in the landscape architecture program at Berkeley. Tetlow's concerns included the entrances to the Common: the path from Greenwood Terrace and the northern access drive. He also expressed the need for a sense of unity for the houses facing the Common. He appreciated the position of the existing walks but thought that the plant material used for the southeast corner of the Common might differ from that used elsewhere. Tetlow suggested leveling the slight slope between lots 6 and 7 to diminish the sense of the Common's sloping into lot 7.[73]

A month after the meeting with Tetlow, Morley Baer wrote to Halprin telling him that he had been selected to plan the landscape of the common areas. The letter of appointment informed him that committee members were to submit their suggestions for the completion of the project.[74] A letter from Ann Birge to Halprin followed, indicating the committee's acceptance of grass as the groundcover, and welcoming further suggestions for discussion at their October 5, 1955, meeting. The program as laid out at the June meeting included the following requirements, revealing the intended cooperative use of the space by all the residents.

1.   The plan should be simple in form, and an open feeling should be maintained.
2.   Native plants should be used; these would not require irrigation once established.
3.   The selected groundcover should keep the adobe soil from cracking.
4.   Some area, assigned to children's play, should be left without planting. Although there would be no play equipment at present, a play sculpture or large wooden stumps might be considered in the future. Swings were considered unsuitable.
5.   Some area should be available for adult relaxation with book and blanket.
6.   Definite plans should be made for replanting the existing pine trees.
7.   The plan should be designed to carry well into the future.
8.   Better use of the parking area should be made than at present, but a parking area should not extend more than a few feet farther into the Common.
9.   A walk from the parking area to the center of the Common is needed, with a ramp replacing or augmenting the existing steps to the Common.
10. From the start, funds should be set aside for maintaining the plantings while they are getting established.[75]

Wurster's original idea sited the north rank of houses at the rear of their lots, to maximize the garden spaces facing the Common, which raised the question of whether Halprin should develop a uniform planting scheme for the properties on the

[L-4] *opposite above*
LAWRENCE HALPRIN, SITE PLAN, 1955.
A ROW OF PLUM TREES, GEOMETRIC SPACES, AND PATHS SHAPE THE SHARED COMMON SPACE.
[EDA, UCB]

[L-5] *opposite below*
LAWRENCE HALPRIN, THE COMMON AREA, PERSPECTIVE, 1956.
ENTRANCE IS THROUGH THE PLUM ALLÉE BETWEEN THE BLAISDELL HOUSE AND LOT #6, LEFT UNBUILT.
[ARCHITECTURAL ARCHIVES, UNIVERSITY OF PENNSYLVANIA, HEREAFTER AA, UP]

north side of the driveway. Sadly, a uniform plan was mooted: northside properties became isolated from the Common by tall fences that created individual gardens for each of the homes and provided privacy from the public areas as well as the intended homes on lots 5 and 6. In the end, of course, these lots remained unbuilt, expanding the open space and the fences, although assuring privacy, became barriers to views of and access to the Common [figure L-6].

Of equal concern as the trees and scheduling was the cost. Three ideas for funding the work were proposed: (1) slow development, involving no extra assessments, with the plan approved the first year, grading during the next year, etc.; (2) an extra assessment requiring unanimous approval that would provide for the entire development in a single year; or (3) an extra assessment for starting the development and finishing it gradually without further assessments. The vote on the best option was postponed until completion of the preliminary plan.[76]

The minutes of the October 1955 annual membership meeting raised several interesting reflections on the relationships among the residents as both homeowners and members of a corporation. For example, the membership chose to emphasize the individual owners' responsibilities toward the community, which included, that as individuals their property should contribute toward the harmonious appearance of the entire site. They also agreed that acting cooperatively could be cost efficient; that is, if members would contribute their labor, the grass and sprinklers could be installed at only a small cost. They also followed Halprin's suggestion that they save money by using a "college boy" rather than a landscape gardener to mow the grass and water the area, and that supervision could be rotated among members at six-month intervals.[77]

[L-6]
VIEW OF COMMON LOOKING WEST FROM THE BIRGE HOUSE.
[MORLEY BAER, UCSC]

Early on, complaints about the weeds and shrubs growing on the undeveloped lots 5 and 6 resulted in a letter to Mr. Thornberg living on an adjacent lot on La Loma Street, requesting him to trim the hedge along the east end of his property and to clear weeds at least twice a year. The importance of the view and openness was stressed, while acknowledging that maintenance should be as simple as possible. The minutes record that trees other than just the pines and flowering plums should be considered, and that Mr. Halprin should suggest how the owners of individual lots could create landscapes that would foster a unity of appearance, especially along Rose Street.[78]

The initial designs included a fountain to be constructed on the Common. Halprin considered a fountain "a funny thing to have in the Common," a thought he later recalled as a topic of numerous discussions. Would a fountain enhance the area or create a problem? And what about funds for its upkeep? There were also safety concerns, for example, the potential of children falling into it.[79] That the fountain was never constructed enhances the landscape's feeling of natural timelessness rather than it's grounding in a specific era [figure L-7].

Halprin's designs were based on the likelihood that the central lots would be developed. His plan proposed a biomorphic oval filled with grass set at the end of the plum allée between the Maenchen (lot 10) and Baer (lot 7) homes [figure L-8]. A paved path tracing the edge of the Baer fence led to the parking lot to the north; the fountain would have stood in the curve where the oval path joined the path to the parking lot. Four benches provided places to rest along the oval path; lighting marked the way at night. A redwood bulkhead would define the boundary of the central area and serve

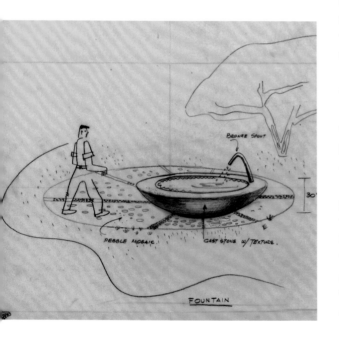

[L-7]
LAWRENCE HALPRIN,
FOUNTAIN DESIGN, c. 1956.
[AA, UP]

[L-8] *below*
**LAWRENCE HALPRIN,
GREENWOOD COMMON
LANDSCAPE PLAN,
NO DATE.**
[AA, UP]

[L-9] *opposite above*
**SAMUEL SCHAAF AND NEPHEWS
PLAYING FOOTBALL, 1962.**
[COURTESY LAURA SCHAAF]

[L-10] *opposite below*
**GREENWOOD GAZETTE,
ANN ACKERMAN, EDITOR.**
"NEWSPAPER" PUT OUT BY
CHILDREN OF THE FAMILIES
LIVING ON GREENWOOD COMMON,
c. 1960.
[MORLEY BAER, UCSC]

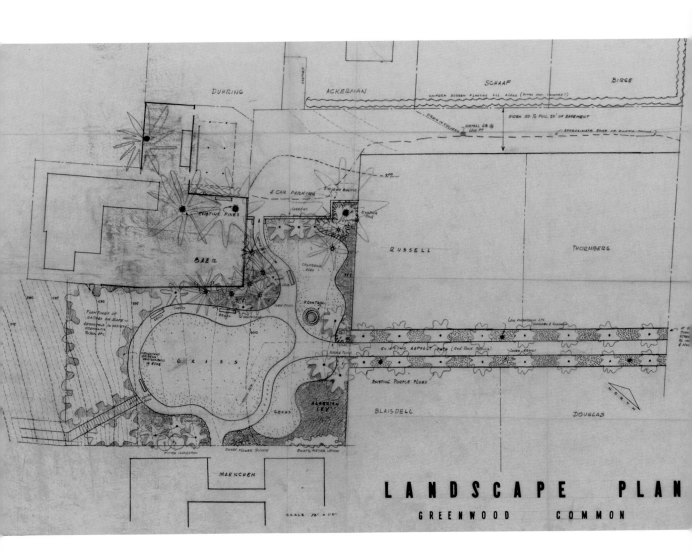

as the retaining wall between the Common and the parking lot.

Algerian ivy covered the ground westward from the Blaisdell residence, extending across the undeveloped central lots to the Maenchen house [figure L-9]. Grass softened the areas surrounding and within the paved oval. On the western edge of the Common, Halprin proposed native plants for the slope including ceanothus, fremontia, and toyon. A row of peach trees along the north side of the access road was included in Halprin's overall plan.

The design as completed and implemented reflected both the needs of the residents and a respect for the site. Retaining the Monterey pines, the simple elegance of the plum allée, the central lawn, and the choice and placement of the native and low-maintenance plants combined an unpretentious yet near-perfect relationship between home and collective landscape [figure L-10].

When asked about the process of designing the landscape for Greenwood Common in a 2005 interview, Halprin remembered having less engagement in the discussions with the client group than he would have in later years.[80] He also recalled that Wurster was very much involved through informal telephone calls. In retrospect, Halprin credited the idea of Greenwood Common and the ideas he acquired on the kibbutz as influencing his concepts for the common areas at The Sea Ranch.[81]

During the first decade of its existence, the Common owners shared the gardening chores on a rotating basis with specific owners assigned responsibility for boundaries related to their individual properties. Although everyone took their turns at cutting, watering, and planting grass, Mrs. Douglas cared for the hedge on the south side of the path in front of both her house and the one

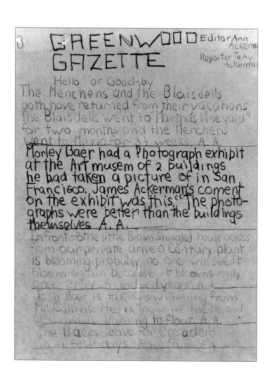

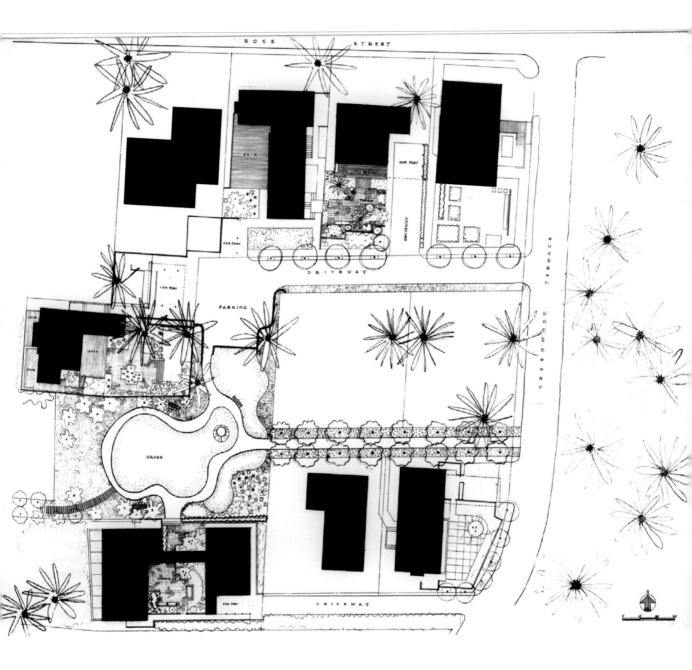

[L-11]

GREENWOOD COMMON SITE PLAN SHOWING GARDENS DESIGNED BY LAWRENCE HALPRIN, c. 1958.

[LAWRENCE HALPRIN, AA, UP; DUHRING AND BIRGE HOUSES ADDED BY MATTHEW GUÈREÑA, 2008]

beside it [figure L-11]. The Baers maintained the areas adjoining their fence and the slope of lot 12.[82] Over time, hired gardeners, whose fees were figured into the annual assessment, assumed what had originally been the members' personal chores. Issues, including labor costs and tree trimming to maintain views, were decided by discussions at meetings. On occasion, weekend work parties were held, and these became neighborly events that generally ended with a group picnic.

The minutes of the October 1960 meeting provide a glimpse into the personalities of the members. They reveal that "Mr. Baer reported that the White Can Company insisted that his can be carried out to Greenwood Terrace once a week so he told them to take their can and keep it."[83] They also illustrate the Common's ongoing relationships with Wurster, as both founder and neighbor, and with Halprin. At this meeting it was determined that Baer, with Wurster and the City of Berkeley, would explore the idea of additional lighting on Greenwood Terrace, and with Halprin additional lights near the parking area and the Maenchen property.

The history of the central lots plays an important part in the history of the Common landscape. From the beginning, they served as a community gathering place. [figures L-12, L-13]. In 1964, the board responded enthusiastically to the Russells' proposed consultation with a Mr. Lindstrom for the extensive landscaping of their central lots. This inspired the Board to review the master plans to develop ways of including landscape work that would be executed on the central lots.

Future activities already guided by the master plan included planting new pines near the Russell lots, installing a gate on the Greenwood Terrace

[L-12]
GROUNDCOVERS AND IVY SHAPE THE CENTRAL AREA OF THE COMMON.
[MARC TREIB, 2007]

entrance, and replacing or removing the row of peach trees that grew in front of the fences along the northern service road. Two years of the trees' leaf curl and their need for trimming and picking up their fallen fruit led to their removal. They were never replaced.

Ongoing discussions during the 1960s and 70s raised the issue of replacing the lawn with another groundcover to reduce financial outlay, and in the early 1970s, to respond to the drought that California then suffered.[84] In the end, the decision to retain the lawn always won. Again, in 1974, the landscape committee responded to the need to upgrade and unify the landscape by creating a list of objectives and activities. Included among these were retaining Halprin's original design concept, the visual enhancement of the Common, selection of new plants for their hardiness, require-ments of minimal maintenance, and compatibility with existing plants. Other ideas included consulting with the Duhring's landscape architect—unnamed, but presumably Geraldine Knight Scott—about aggressively trimming and pruning to restore the sense of the Common, opening views from north to south, and enhancing privacy by relocating shrubs and bushes along the Greenwood Terrace street edge.[85]

Clearly the 1977 purchase of the central lots required that the landscape master plan be revisited. The landscape committee and other members met with landscape architect Mai Arbegast to create a plan that would integrate new ideas with those of the original landscape plan. The first order of business was to address planting for the central areas. Recommendations included removing the ivy planted between the old Common and the new lots, removal and/or pruning of bushes and trees,

[L-13]

RESIDENTS WALKING THROUGH THE PLUM ALLÉE.
[COURTESY SB MASTER]

and planting a row of trees—Japanese flowering crabapple trees alternating with flowering cherries —on the north side of the property to match the spacing of the plum allée to the south, as the peach trees had previously done.

Landscape design, like maintenance, is a continuing process. According to some second-generation residents, an unidentified person planted —independently—a row of three large agapanthus across the lawn to discourage running dogs and children playing Frisbee and touch football. To maintain a strongly defined boundary between the Common and Greenwood Terrace, property owners had relied on the simple device of a hedge almost from the start. By the mid-eighties, the hedge was failing and a fence was constructed as its replacement. In 1983 the landscape committee met with landscape architect Patricia O'Brien to find solutions for fixing the various paved surfaces and to develop a new master plan that could be implemented in phases. In response to a family of deer living just beyond the ridge to the west, more recent landscaping required deer resistant flowering shrubs such as salvias and lavenders. [figure L14].

[L-14]

THE WINDING PATHS AT THE WEST-ERN EDGE OF THE COMMON, WITH THE MAENCHEN HOUSE BEYOND.

[CRIS BENTON, 2008]

Part 3:
The Houses

Birge Residence

1 Greenwood Common; 1955, 1966

Client:
Robert & Ann Birge

Architect:
Donald Olsen

"It was the only one of my houses that wasn't painted white."[86]

The two-story Birge residence, sited on the northeast corner of Greenwood Common, is entered over a bridge from Greenwood Terrace [figure 1-1]. Unlike other residences on the north side of the Common that match in height the single-story houses across the green, the Birge house rides boldly on its raised second story, giving a commanding view of the Common, the bay, and the Golden Gate in the distance. Curiously, it is the only house with a living room that has a view to the Common itself. The site was originally the Gregorys' tennis court, and in fact, during construction, pieces of asphalt had to be removed while excavating for foundations and future planting [figure 1-2].[87]

That the Birges would build their home on the Common was no surprise. Bob Birge grew up on nearby La Vereda Street; as a boy he rode his bicycle along Greenwood Terrace and picked blackberries in a field to the west. Ann Birge's parents were close friends of the parents of Jack Kent, founder of Berkeley's planning department, and must have been aware of the community of planners and designers then active in the area.[88]

In 1952, intrigued by the proposed division of the Greenwood property, Birge asked Wurster to add his name to the list of potential purchasers; he became number 22. Despite the long odds, a year later he was asked to choose between lots 1 and 4. He chose lot 1: it offered the best access to both Rose Street and Greenwood Terrace plus the potential for height-related views. Traditional financing was a challenge

55

[1-2]
BIRGE RESIDENCE, SOUTH YARD.
NOTE TENNIS COURT LINES.
[BOB SKELTON; EDA, UCB]

[1-3]
**DONALD OLSEN, KIP RESIDENCE,
BERKELEY, 1952.**
[EDA, UCB]

as "no bank wanted to finance buying a lot that required $5000 for the land and $1000 for a share of the Common." However, he and his wife managed to purchase their lot in 1952 after securing a loan from the Federal Housing Administration; foundation-digging started two years later.[89]

The Birges, then living on Parker Street in Berkeley, began the process of selecting their architect—Wurster preferred not to recommend specific designers. As physicists, they had known the physicist Arthur Kip in Cambridge and visited him in California after his return to Berkeley in 1951. Kip was partial to modern design and had built a home in a community of Gropius disciples while in Massachusetts.[90]

Once settled in Berkeley in 1952, Kip hired architect Donald Olsen to design a house for him in the modernist International Style, and the Birges' experience of Kip's house led them to select Olsen as their architect [figure 1-3]. In a 2005 interview, Bob Birge acknowledged that: "I hired him as an artist."[91]

Donald Olsen, an unwavering advocate of the International Style, graduated in 1942 from the University of Minnesota with a B.A. in architecture, and in 1946 earned his Master's from the Graduate School of Design at Harvard University. He then worked both independently and with several firms, including Saarinen, Swanson & Saarinen; Skidmore, Owings & Merrill; and Wurster, Bernardi, & Emmons. He opened his own practice in 1953. In 1954 he designed his own home next to Arthur Kip's in the same modernist style. He taught in the architecture school at the University of California between 1960 and 1990, and was chosen by Wurster as one of the team of designers, with Joseph Esherick and Vernon DeMars, for Wurster Hall, the new home of the university's College of Environmental Design, which was completed in 1964.

The Birge house was to be a square living space raised on columns above two carports and storage areas. Olsen had used the concept before and would return to it throughout his career. In 1949, for example, he had designed a weekend residence for Archie McLelland in Sausalito [figure 1-4]. Here too, metal posts supported a living space above a carport. The Birge house is a modified and expanded version of this earlier design, but here Olsen balanced his preferred hard-edged vocabulary with the softer, more natural, regional aesthetic preferred by Wurster and the residents of the Common. In a 1952 letter he suggested that "the best and most economical plan for the house would be a single story arrangement at ground level. However, because of the potentialities of your site in respect to the view, I feel it worthwhile to spend some time investigating the possibilities of a plan which would elevate the living room above ground level [figures 1-5, 1-6].[92]

After submitting his first scheme Olsen left for travel in Europe, leaving his colleague Alvin Fingado to supervise the Birge project.[93] When he returned, it was with new ideas and "a whole new and better plan."[94] "I am taking this opportunity to approach the design with a fresh start," he wrote, suggesting that the Birges "try not to carry over particular items from the past design into a new one…because any new design must reach its own balance."[95] His new plan had an enlarged residential footprint that

[1-4]
DONALD OLSEN, McLELLAND RESIDENCE, SAUSALITO, 1949.
[EDA, UCB]

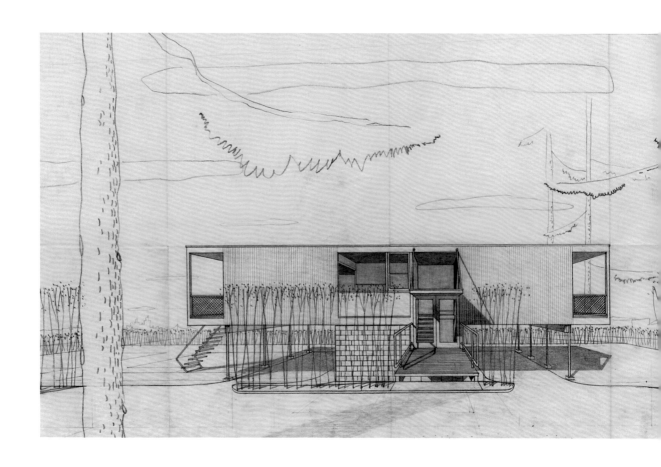

[1-5] *opposite*
BIRGE RESIDENCE,
CONCEPTUAL SKETCHES, 1952.
〔EDA, UCB〕

[1-6] *above*
BIRGE RESIDENCE, PERSPECTIVE.
〔EDA, UCB〕

included a larger kitchen—but not so large as to "result in diminishing efficiency"—and bedrooms with dimensions sufficient for beds more than seven feet long. The change challenged the clients' serious cost limitations but was accepted nonetheless [figure 1-7].

The house as constructed is a wood-frame, rectangular box lifted on steel pipe columns, with additional support provided by concrete-block walls that enclose the mechanical and storage spaces. Set eight feet off the ground to gain views of San Francisco Bay, the east and west elevations are divided into three distinct sections bordered by cantilevered decks to the north and south sides. Stained-wood siding, laid vertically and punctured with windows set asymmetrically, comprise the entry façade. Originally the outside trim was painted green but Olsen, displeased with the effect, had it repainted black.

A bridge connects the entrance to Greenwood Terrace. A wooden canopy both protects and compresses the entry at the front door. Its low ceiling contrasts dramatically with the thirteen-foot ceilings of the interior entry hall and enhances the sense of opening—a spatial effect frequently used by architects such as Frank Lloyd Wright to manipulate the transition between interior and exterior spaces. The canopy punctuates the tall glass wall set back in the center of the wood-faced exterior, adding a third dimension to the façade and balancing the bridge below it [see figure 1-1].

On either side of the entry, the irregularity of the windows indicates different functions within—although not with complete clarity: to the left of the entry, large windows signal

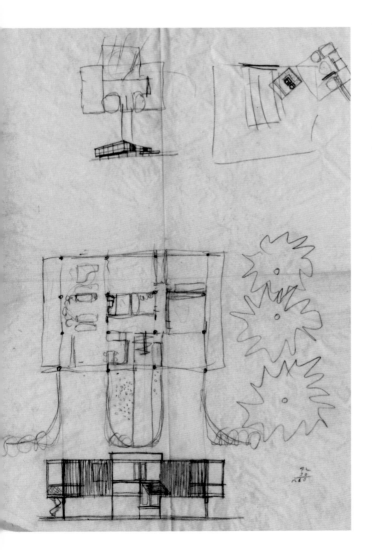

[1-7]
BIRGE RESIDENCE, PLAN AND EAST ELEVATION STUDIES, 1954.
[EDA, UCB]

a public room whereas in actuality they light the kitchen, while the dining room is set behind the solid wall. The vertical fenestration of the entry's north wall accurately suggests a more private, or secondary, space; in fact, the room behind it is private: a bedroom. A full-length deck, accessible from two of the three rooms on the bedroom side of the house, extends the interior spaces to the north. On the south side a second deck provides a symmetrical counterpoint [figure 1-8].

The plan is essentially a square divided into nine equally sized modules—a Palladian planning device. That same year Olsen used the device for his own home [figure 1-9]. The Birge living/dining room combined three units of the square into a large rectangular space; the center section contained the family room, bathrooms, hallway, and kitchen; three bedrooms on the north side completed the cube. The lower floor held mechanical equipment and a small bathroom in the center with carports on either side. A wide staircase in the entrance hall leads to the living spaces, and to the right, a narrower stair descends to the lower level [figure 1-10].

A fireplace centered in the north wall—cleanly built with no protruding mantle—provides the focal point for the living room, whose south wall of windows gives visual access to the wooden deck, the garden, and the Common beyond. Exposed structural beams and wood planks form the ceiling, complementing the mahogany paneling of the walls [figure 1-11]. Four years after the house was completed, the Birges worked with Olsen again to convert the "west room"—originally a family room—into a

[1-8]
BIRGE RESIDENCE, VIEW FROM THE NORTHWEST.
[BOB SKELTON, 1955; EDA, UCB]

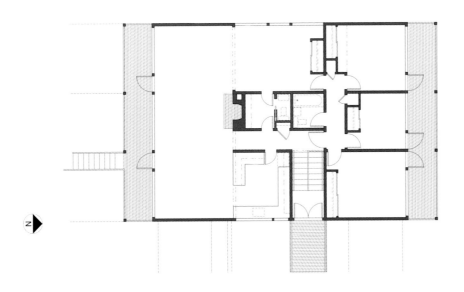

[1-9] *above*
**DONALD OLSEN, OLSEN RESIDENCE,
BERKELEY, 1954. FLOOR PLAN.**
THE PRECEDENT FOR BIRGE
RESIDENCE
[EDA,UCB]

[1-10] *below*
**BIRGE RESIDENCE,
MAIN FLOOR PLAN.**
[MATTHEW GUËREÑA, 2008]

[1-11]
BIRGE RESIDENCE, LIVING ROOM.
[BOB SKELTON, c. 1956; EDA, UCB]

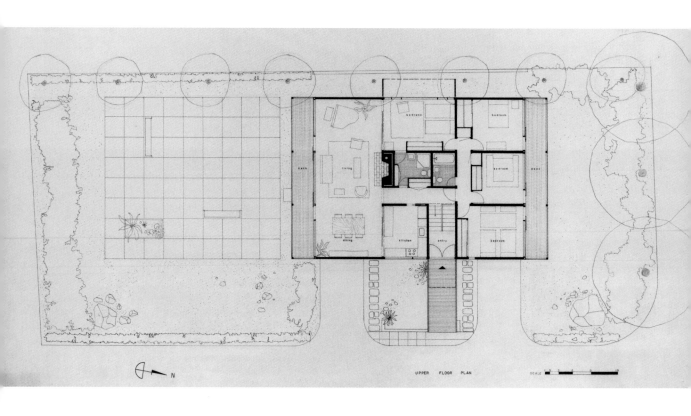

UPPER FLOOR PLAN   SCALE

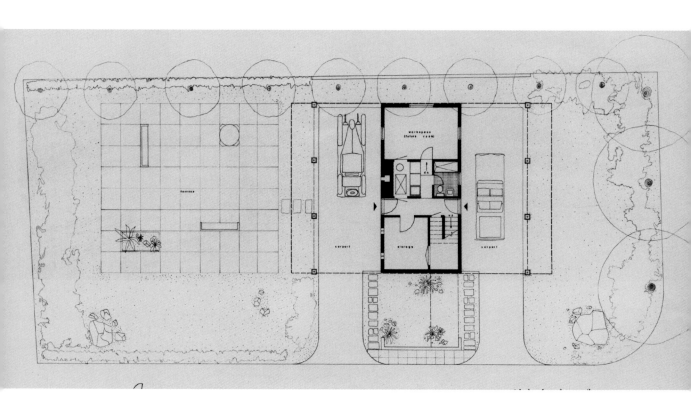

new master bedroom. At this time Olsen proposed a freestanding storage unit—with as "many drawers as possible"—on the new wall separating this bedroom from the living room.

In 1966 Olsen enclosed the south carport, converting it into a playroom, snack area, and laundry area [figure 1-12]. Alterations at that time also changed the lower floor bathroom, bedroom, and corridor. The north carport was also enclosed, for security—the Birges had been bothered by the crowds attending Grateful Dead concerts at the university's nearby Greek Theater.[96]

From the beginning, Olsen's design for the south façade included a garden and patio area although only a patch of grass on the drawings suggested where it might be located. The architect also proposed three minor garden elements: on the north side, a simple yard shaded by three large trees and bordered by hedges for privacy along Rose Street; to the west, a row of nine smaller trees masking the fence at the property line; and as an approach to the front door, a small lawn was bordered by paving and several plants [figure 1-13].

The main garden, set south of the house, took form as a paved square with lawn on two sides and shrubs to screen it from view. It is interesting to compare plans showing Olsen's vision of the garden with photographs of the garden as realized. Asphalt vestiges of the Gregory tennis courts remained visible [see figure 1-2]. In its initial configuration the borders of this area were planted and six framed beds laid out. In a 1955 letter, Olsen strongly suggested that the Birges should hire a landscape architect and that he would be pleased to make recom-

mendations.[97] But none were consulted. In 1973, most of the south garden was displaced by a swimming pool and a tall fence. The latter replaced a low fence with a gate in the southwest corner that had accessed the Common.

The commanding presence of this house both defines the eastern boundary of the Common and serves as a counterpoint to the Maenchen residence to the west. Its natural wood and glass exterior and asymmetrical elements signal the modernist design aesthetic found throughout the development.

[1-12]
BIRGE RESIDENCE, MAIN FLOOR AND SITE PLAN, 1954.
[EDA, UCB]

[1-13]
BIRGE RESIDENCE, GROUND FLOOR AND SITE PLAN, 1954.
[EDA, UCB]

Schaaf Residence

2 Greenwood Common, 1957

Client:
Samuel & Phyllis Schaaf

Architect:
Robert Klemmedson

Landscape Architect:
Lawrence Halprin

The Schaaf house, whose construction began in 1956, was the last house built on the Common [figure 2-1]. In the late 1940s, Samuel and Phyllis Schaaf hired Robert Klemmedson to design an L-shaped ranch style house in Orinda. However Mrs. Schaaf, who had been raised in Oakland, hated the heat in Orinda and wanted to return to a more maritime climate.[98] So after only a few years in their Orinda home, the Schaafs bought their lot at Greenwood Common, and as early as 1954 were corresponding with their future neighbor Robert Birge about technical matters such as the proper placement of sewer pipes. During the design and construction of their house on Greenwood Common, they rented a house nearby on La Loma Street.

Professor Schaaf taught mechanical engineering at the University of California, Berkeley; Mrs. Schaaf audited art history and architecture classes and took an active interest in the design and construction of the new house. She wanted a "timber Berkeley-type house with no hallways and lots of closets:" one that was different than their Orinda house constructed with too many hallways.[99] The proximity of their temporary quarters facilitated her time on the construction site as the house was built.

Robert Klemmedson's education in architecture began at the University of California, Berkeley, in 1940 but World War II intervened with a tour of duty in the Pacific Theatre, followed by a posting in Japan during the occupation. It was there he acquired an interest in Japanese architecture that informed his designs throughout his practice. Once back home he continued his schooling, then opened a practice in Orinda.

[2-1]
**ROBERT KLEMMEDSON,
SCHAAF RESIDENCE,
GREENWOOD COMMON,
BERKELEY, 1957.**
VIEWED FROM THE COMMON.
[MORLEY BAER, UCSC; c. 1958]

The Schaaf house, with its lower floor hidden from the Common, appears to be one story. At the time the house was designed, Rose Street was a busy thoroughfare. In response, the house was positioned in the middle of the lot despite losing the potential for a larger garden area had the house been set further to the north [figure 2-2].

Despite the modern movement's romance with the flat roof, three of the houses on the Common have sloped-roofs: the two on the north side align their ridges on an east-west line, parallel to the access road. In the Schaaf house, the ridge is not set in the center of the floor plan but reaches its highest point above the kitchen and dining area, sloping quickly to the north deck and slowly over the living room to the garden. The roof planes horizontally overlap the carport / entrance creating a dynamic interaction with the vertical fence [figure 2-3]. From the Common, little of the house, clad with resawn redwood siding, is visible, hidden as it is by a slat fence that encloses the garden.

The north side of the house receives little sun but two decks nonetheless give access to the outdoors from the dining area and the bedrooms on both floors. The decks are also accessible by exterior stairs on the east side [figure 2-4]. An intriguing system of hinged plywood and screened ventilation panels above all the doors and windows on this side of the house can be opened when needed.

The simple exterior and low building profile give no clue to the comfortable and surprising open plan within: far from any restrained arrangement of the interior spaces, one encounters a panoply of planes and varied heights, shapes, and color. Mrs. Schaaf insisted

[2-2]
SCHAAF RESIDENCE, CONSTRUCTION PHOTO, 1957.
[COURTESY LAURA SCHAAF]

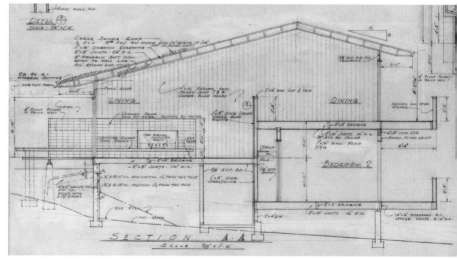

[2-3]
SCHAAF RESIDENCE, DRIVEWAY, CARPORT AND ENTRANCE.
[MORLEY BAER, UCSC]

[2-4]
SCHAAF RESIDENCE, SECTION, CONSTRUCTION DRAWING, 1957.
[COURTESY KLEMMEDSON & KLEMMEDSON ARCHITECTS]

that the house should have no hallways—and there are none. The entry foyer leads into a large living room with a fireplace set against a solid, wood-sheathed wall to the west and a fully glazed south wall giving onto a deck that overlooks the garden [figure 2-5]. The hearth is a lightly colored, polished concrete slab surrounded by a panel of white brick and capped with a redwood board that serves as a mantle. Both the brick fireplace wall and the concrete hearth extend through the exterior glass wall into the garden—an intriguing detail that joins inside and out.

From the lower level of the living room, the space expands through succeeding layers of wall planes. The sweeping pitched roof and exposed rafters, reflect the architect's interest in Japanese design. The ceiling uses wooden boards of differing lengths beautifully fitted together. According to family members, the contractor John Kay "went crazy trying to match the colors as he pieced together the redwood boards on the ceiling."[100] The twelve-to-fourteen-foot ceiling embraces both the living room and raised dining room of the split level interior, allowing an openness in all the public spaces that also promotes social interaction: the short dining room wall allows those in the living room to converse with diners [figure 2-6]. A pass-through wall of open shelves separates the dining room from the kitchen on this upper level, which also includes a guest room and bath. An exposed stovepipe painted a light terracotta orange rising to the peaked ceiling contributed to the playful coziness of the interiors [figures 2-7A, 7B].

[2-5]
**SCHAAF RESIDENCE,
LIVING ROOM.**
THE FIREPLACE SURROUND
CONTINUES AS A GARDEN WALL.

[MARC TREIB, 2008]

On the lower level, glass walls in each room give onto the long balconies that look to the greenery and to Rose Street beyond. Between these bedrooms are mirror-image bathrooms with a shared sunken tub. Mrs. Schaaf, always interested in classical architecture, traveled with her family to Italy in 1955, visiting Rome and Hadrian's Villa on their journey. Family legend has it that it was this trip that stimulated the wish for a sunken tub—which they always referred to as the Roman Bath.[101]

The garden design was initiated at the same time as the house construction.[102] Lawrence Halprin remembered that he met the Schaafs while working on the broader plan for the Common landscape in July 1957.[103] A year later, the Halprin office expressed concern about the way the Schaafs were intending to plant their site and asked that the Schaafs "get all the plants and supervise their installation rather than put them in piecemeal"—it was "important to compose the entire garden as a picture rather than put in isolated plants and then try and make them relate."[104] The garden was constructed later that fall.[105]

Unlike other gardens on the north side of the Common, its original design used a fence to enclose a personal garden and probably to give privacy from the homes expected at the time to be constructed on lots 5 and 6 [figure 2-8].[106] The other homes bordering the access road added fences for similar reasons but later, after their initial construction.

Two staggered brick patios accommodate varying functions. The patio closer to the house was originally planned for conversion to a

[2-6]
SCHAAF RESIDENCE, LIVING ROOM WITH DINING BALCONY ABOVE.
[MARC TREIB, 2008]

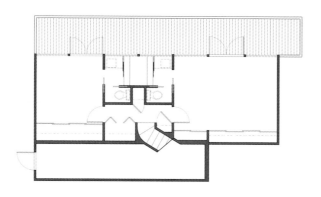

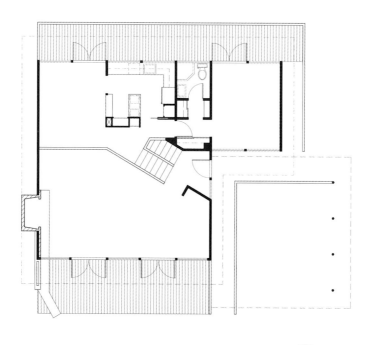

[2-7A, 7B]
SCHAAF RESIDENCE, LOWER AND UPPER FLOOR PLANS.
[MATTHEW GUËREÑA, 2008]

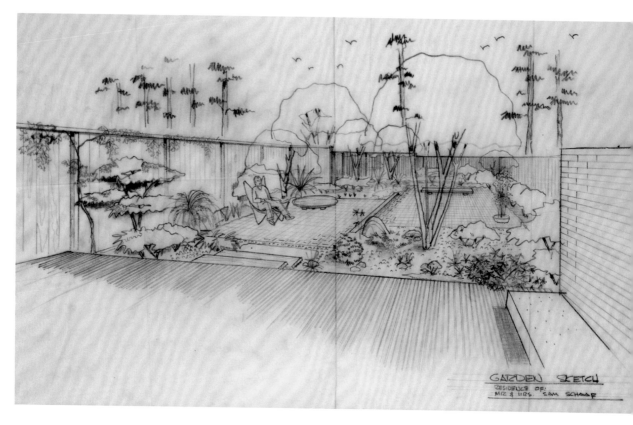

GARDEN SKETCH
RESIDENCE OF:
MR & MRS. SAM SCHAAF

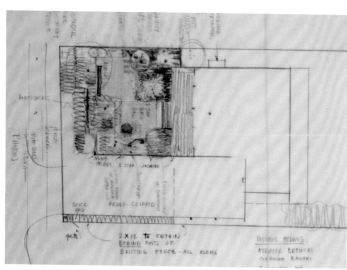

[2-8]
LAWRENCE HALPRIN,
SCHAAF GARDEN.
PERSPECTIVE SKETCH, c. 1958.
[AA, UP]

[2-9]
SCHAAF GARDEN, PLANTING
PLAN, c. 1958.
[AA, UP]

swimming pool that was never built. Low shrubs, fruit trees, evergreens, flowering plants, and an herb garden enclose the area and give color and a sense of seasonal change—particularly brilliant in springtime when the flowering cherry trees bloom. It is clear from the planting plan that shaded areas and color were important elements of the design [figure 2-9]. A Virginia creeper still climbs the outer wall of the fireplace, while a pittosporum shades the deck and guarantees privacy. An herb garden graced by lavender, rosemary, and thyme once filled the southwest corner of the garden [figure 2-10].

The juniper was included in the original plant list as was a Monterey pine, later removed when it grew too tall.[107] Flowering shrubs, a magnolia, jasmine, wisteria, and either a birch or dogwood close to the house filled out the eastern edge of the site and container plants energized the garden and deck with spots of color. Wisteria was encouraged to cover the fence at the entrance, extending along the front of the carport to hide the roofline. The garden was much used by the family over their years of occupancy and continues to offer glorious color in both the spring and fall [figure 2-11].

Plans for a north, or rear, garden were begun in fall 1958 but never carried out. For this space Halprin had proposed a narrow, sloping garden whose central feature was a patio of red rock [figure 2-12]. A large Monterey pine, later removed because it blocked too much light making the house "dark and gloomy," stymied the plan's execution. After its removal Mrs. Schaaf planted pittosporum and other tall shrubs to serve as a living fence that would shield the house from busy Rose Street further down the hillside.[108] As a result, the back garden was neither developed nor really used.

Hidden behind a slat fence, this house is a delightful surprise. Constructed in 1957, the elegant informality of the Schaaf house preceded by nearly a decade the open plan, multi-layered playful residences that were later designed for The Sea Ranch, a community of single family houses on the Sonoma County coast nestled in a Halprin-designed environment [figure 2-13].

[2-10]
**LAWRENCE HALPRIN,
SCHAAF GARDEN.**
VIEWED FROM THE DECK.
[MORLEY BAER, UCSC; c. 1959,]

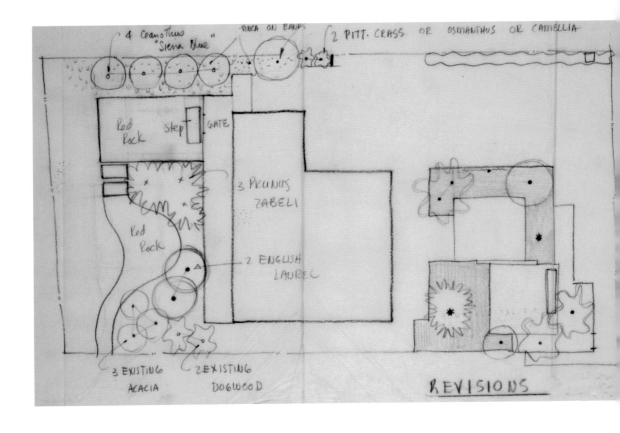

[2-11] *above*
**LAWRENCE HALPRIN,
SCHAAF GARDEN, THE CHERRY
TREES IN BLOOM.**
[COURTESY OF LAURA SCHAAF]

[2-12] *below*
**SCHAAF GARDEN, REAR GARDEN
PLAN, NO DATE.**
[AA, UP]

[2-13]
SCHAAF GARDEN.

THE DECK EXTENDS THE INTERIOR
OF THE HOUSE INTO THE GARDEN,
c. 1959.
[MARC TREIB, 2008]

Ackerman Residence

3 Greenwood Common, 1954

Client:
James & Mildred Ackerman

Architect:
Joseph Esherick

Landscape Architect:
Lawrence Halprin

William Wurster hired James Ackerman as the School of Architecture's first full-time architectural historian, an appointment held jointly with the Department of Art beginning in the fall of 1952.[109] It is likely that Ackerman, aware of the quality of his work, sought out Joseph Esherick, his colleague in the Department of Architecture, to design his new home [figure 3-1]. According to James Ackerman, the house:

> was built under some pressure. In 1952 we were living on Buena Vista Way in a cutesy French Provincial oddity when my wife, who had just started teaching dance at Mills [College], got polio in the last big epidemic. The house was a total frustration to a person in a wheelchair. So #3 [Greenwood Common] was built for optimal movement for her. We lived there only three, maybe 4 years and sold it for $40,000, about what it had cost originally. Joe [Esherick] complained that apart from wheelchair issues we didn't give him enough rules to conform to, that there wasn't a definite form or environment in our minds; I guess for my part, the discipline of historical scholarship had a distancing effect as well as a desire not to get in the way of the inventive process, even if such gettings-in-the-way were important to the architect's definitions.[110]

This project arrived just as Esherick's career was hitting its stride. Graduating from the University of Pennsylvania in 1937 with a degree in architecture, he moved to San Francisco the following year where he began working in the office of Gardner Dailey. At the time, Dailey and

[3-1]

JOSEPH ESHERICK, ACKERMAN RESIDENCE, GREENWOOD COMMON, BERKELEY, 1954.

VIEW FROM GREENWOOD COMMON PRIOR TO THE CONSTRUCTION OF THE FENCE.

[LOUIS ALLEY; EDA, UCB]

William Wurster were the two most prominent Bay Area architects then designing in the modern idiom. Following service in World War II, Esherick opened his own San Francisco architectural practice in 1946, partnering over time with George Homsey, Peter Dodge, and Charles Davis. As both a leading local practitioner and faculty member in the architecture department, his work strongly influenced residential design in the Bay Area.[111]

Esherick's determination to come up with the best design for his client and colleague is evident in the number of sketches he created to work through the program. The primary requirement called for a three-bedroom house for a family of four, with all its principal spaces on one level to address Mrs. Ackerman's mobility requirements. Ackerman recognized that "The problem for the designer of dwellings for young people (I was in my mid-30s) in those times when the young could afford to build houses, was how to provide rooms for small kids that would be bearable when they grew older. We left before it could become an issue."[112]

An early proposal from September 1954 placed the carport and entry path in the southeast corner of the site with the house centered on the lot [figure 3-2]. At this stage, the design for the house took form as two offset rectangular spaces perpendicular to the Common: a short one that contained public spaces such as the living and dining rooms, and a longer wing with the family's private rooms. The entrance along a covered walk paralleled the house on the east side, with entry through a hallway that led to the living room. Both the north and south elevations were completely glazed with floor

to ceiling windows [figure 3-3]. The drawing indicates Esherick's intent to bring light into the house and to create both a public space and private rooms that would capture the southern light and partial garden views. Taking advantage of the slope to Rose Street, Esherick formed two rooms on a lower level, one assigned to office space, the other for a guest [figure 3-4].

As the plan developed the public spaces were reoriented, and alternatives were proposed for the dining room and kitchen [figure 3-5]. Esherick also tried to resolve the northwest corner, specifically the number and placement of windows and doors. By this time he was committed to an L-shaped plan that positioned the bedrooms in the long north-south leg, with the living room, dining room, and kitchen placed in the shorter leg set perpendicular to it. The entrance occupied the intersection of the two wings [figure 3-6]. In the final scheme, wood-shingled wall panels, alternating with tall framed windows, replaced the fully glazed walls originally proposed.

At the entrance, a small garden by Lawrence Halprin lies to the right, a beautiful Japanese maple to the left, but dominating the view is the Douglas-fir deck that covers almost all of this part of the site and welcomes visitors to the living room. The red cedar-shingled exterior of the house nods to the wood-clad craftsman-style residences in the surrounding neighborhood [figure 3-7].

The living room of this modest home displays Esherick's talent for elegance and scale as well as his love of fine millwork and handcrafted hardware. Although only eighteen-by-twenty-five feet, the twelve-foot-high ceilings and glass

[3-2] *opposite above*
ACKERMAN RESIDENCE, PRELIMINARY FLOOR PLAN, SEPTEMBER 1954.
[EDA, UCB]

[3-3] *opposite below*
ACKERMAN RESIDENCE, ELEVATION STUDIES, SEPTEMBER 1954.
[EDA, UCB]

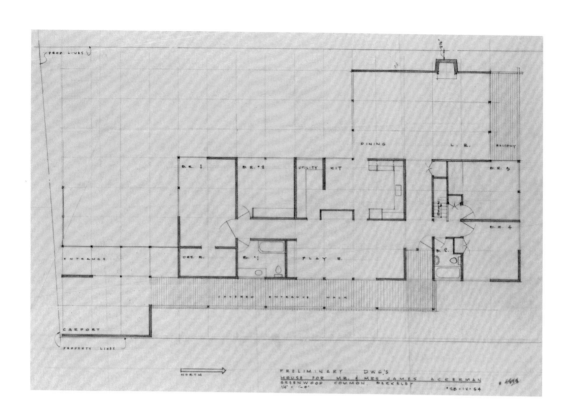

PRELIMINARY DWG'S
HOUSE FOR MR. & MRS. JAMES ACKERMAN
GREENWOOD COMMON, BERKELEY
1/4" = 1'-0"   18 · IX · 54

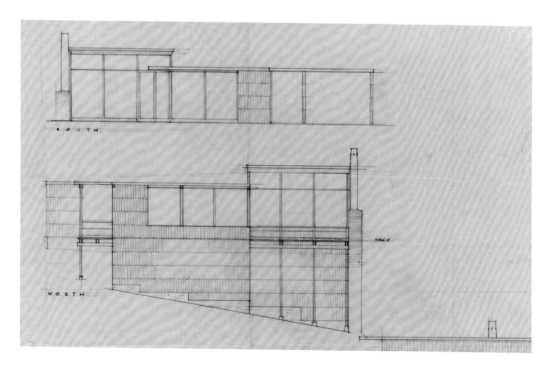

[3-4]
ACKERMAN RESIDENCE, NORTH FAÇADE SEEN FROM ROSE STREET.
THE SLOPE ALLOWED FOR A STUDY AND GUEST ROOM ON THE LOWER FLOOR.
[LOUIS ALLEY; EDA, UCB]

[3-5]
ACKERMAN RESIDENCE, PRELIMINARY FLOOR PLAN, SEPTEMBER 1954.
[EDA, UCB]

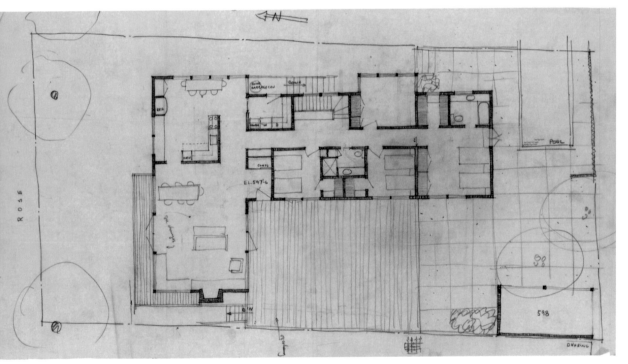

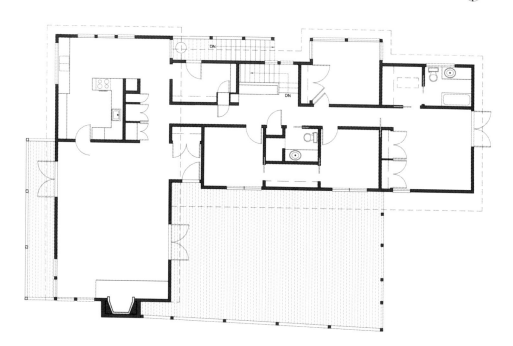

ESHERICK
ACKERMAN

[3-6]
**ACKERMAN RESIDENCE,
FLOOR PLAN.**
[MATTHEW GUÉREÑA, 2008]

doors suggest both the luxury of a large villa and the comfort of an intimate drawing room —a perfect balance that captures what Gardner Dailey saw as the value of the vertical line: it was a "very serene motive."[113] According to Ackerman "the design worked well; the only problem we had was that the frames of the huge double doors onto the deck shrunk from the heat of the sun, and ultimately a substantial space opened up between them."[114] The limits of the material have continued to plague the owners of the home to this day.

The fireplace is deceptively simple: a precast exposed-aggregate concrete hearth with wooden trim that reinforces the horizontal proportions of the room. Esherick, known for his ability to maximize the usefulness and effects of natural light, ultimately wrapped the north-west corner of the living room with large corner windows that also opened views to the west, allowing light to filter through the trees [figure 3-8].

Esherick's attention to detail is evident throughout the house. In the living room, for example, Esherick provided the Ackermans with sufficient wall space to display their collection of paintings by young artists. As Esherick described it:

> what was most refreshing about James Ackerman when he came to the Depart-ment in Berkeley was that he opened up the whole conception about what we were doing, and broadened it, and included painting and sculpture as part of the things that we should be attentive to. He somehow or other got to know emerging painters in the Bay Area, and

> he used to have painters exhibit stuff in his house. Then if you visited him, or had dinner there…or just called on him to look at what was currently on display, you could buy it.[115]

To accommodate Mildred Ackerman's wheelchair, all of the principal living spaces were on the main floor; the hallways and doors were wider than accepted standards; the kitchen was designed with low counters and hanging cabinets, with an open space under the sink and a horizontal refrigerator with doors that slid to the side. Esherick also insured that the kitchen's large glass windows captured the light and the views looking east to the Berkeley Hills.

Changes by the residents who followed the Ackermans have included converting the bedroom nearest the living room into a dining room/foyer with sliding glass doors, installing a skylight in the kitchen, and moving the west wall out by two feet. Professor Willard Farnum enlarged the carport in 1977 and changed the refrigerator to a standard vertical model, shortening the counter, and removing the east-side cabinets to open up the room and bring in yet more light from the windows. In the 1990s, a short flight of external stairs on the east side were relocated to construct a deck containing a hot tub. A later owner extended the hearth to become a window seat, and Esherick admitted that they had improved his house as originally designed.

The garden was designed between 1956 and 1957, like several others by Lawrence Halprin. The early plans proposed a swimming pool outside the master bedroom entered by

[3-7]
ACKERMAN RESIDENCE, ENTRY DECK.
[MARC TREIB]

[3-8]
ACKERMAN RESIDENCE,
LIVING ROOM.
[LOUIS ALLEY; EDA, UCB]

stairs for the children and a slide with bars for Mrs. Ackerman [figure 3-9]. The pool was to be surrounded by a brick patio partly covered by a trellis extending around the house. Notes made early in the project specifically mentioned "no roses, tubs for vines and plants for the deck, a bench on the deck, minimal maintenance required, a service platform and fence on the deck, and an arbor."[116] The final design differed markedly from this early proposal. The pool was never constructed, neither was the arbor nor the brick patio. The deck was extended to cover a good portion of the site, shaded by a large Japanese maple that served as the transition between the entry walk to the house and the garden on the south side [figure 3-10]. A tall gate separating the house from the common was installed by later owners who also removed the original wall to the right of the entrance. This integrated the bedroom garden with the trees and deck. On the north slope of the house, Halprin designed a narrow garden with a cluster of trees on the western end of a winding path running east-west [figure 3-11].

This unassuming house captures essential elements of Esherick's work and midcentury design. The proportions of the living room, sensitivity to the needs of the client, detailing, use of wood throughout the home, and integral placement of light and views provide an understanding of Esherick's gifts. The elegant simplicity of line and function throughout, and the feeling of the single room created when the doors are open between the living room and the deck clearly express the language of California modern living.

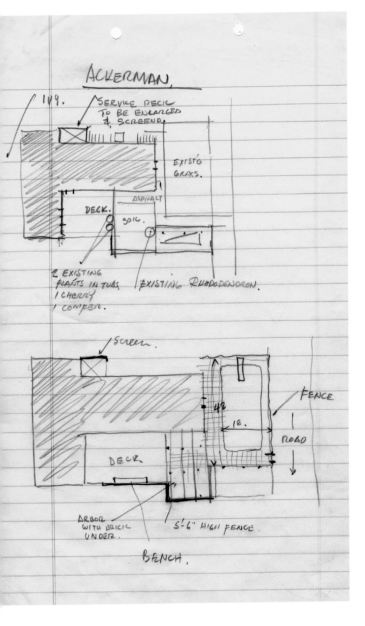

[3-9]
**LAWRENCE HALPRIN, ACKERMAN
GARDEN, PLAN STUDIES, c. 1956.**
[AA, UP]

[3-10]
**ACKERMAN GARDEN,
PERSPECTIVE SKETCH,** c. 1956.

[AA, UP]

[3-11]
**ACKERMAN GARDEN,
PLANTING PLAN,** 1957.

[AA, UP]

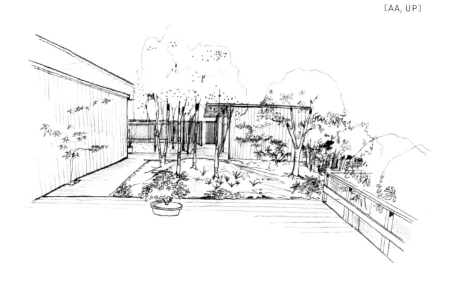

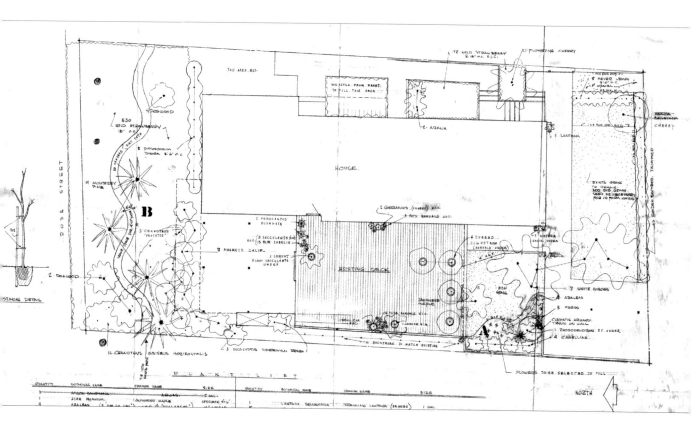

Duhring Residence

4 Greenwood Common, 1954

Client:
Ruth Duhring

Architect:
Harwell Hamilton Harris

Supervising Architect:
Hervey Parke Clark;
Clark & Beuttler, San Francisco

Landscape Architect:
Geraldine Knight Scott

The story of the Duhring residence derives, in part, from local connections. Unlike the other original residents of the Common, Frederick Duhring was not connected to the university. Instead, he had learned of William Wurster and the Greenwood property through his employer, Mason-McDuffie Real Estate. It had been Duhring, in fact, who conducted the property appraisal of the Gregory house and land for Wurster and the Gregory family. And it was through this appraisal that he chose to purchase two of the lots on the Common [figure 4-1].

Harwell Hamilton Harris came to know William Wurster from a letter in which Wurster expressed his admiration for Harris' 1934 Lowe house in Altadena, California. As fellow architects and contemporaries, they shared an interest in both modernity and regionalism. They had jointly escorted the noted Finnish architect Alvar Aalto to see Harris' house for Marion Clark in Carmel on one of his visits to California.[117] The social and architectural critic Lewis Mumford, also a friend of Wurster's, included both architects among the group he credited with defining the Bay Region Style— a humanistic approach to architecture that responded to regional conditions using appropriate materials rather than the more industrial aesthetic favored by some modernist architects.[118]

The Duhrings were also acquainted with Weston Havens, an investment counselor who in 1941 had commissioned Harwell Harris to design his iconic residence in the hills southeast of the campus in Berkeley. In fact, it was this acquaintance that led to Harris being selected by Mrs. Duhring to design her house on the Common [figure 4-2].[119]

[4-1]
**HARWELL HAMILTON HARRIS,
DUHRING RESIDENCE, GREENWOOD
COMMON, BERKELEY, 1954.**
VIEW OF ENTRY STAIRS BETWEEN
GARAGE AND KITCHEN GARDEN
FENCE LEADING TO FRONT DOOR.
[MARC TREIB]

Thus begins a long and arduous trail of letters from Ruth Duhring to Harris. The design and realization of the house was not to be an easy journey. Most of her passive-aggressive and undated letters expressed definite opinions, included endless lists of questions, or suggested changes to her project—although these often closed with a humble admission of uncertainty and belief in his judgment. This first letter sets the tone for those that follow:

> I always enjoy Weston's house when I am there and have liked the pictures of other houses which you have designed. However, Weston's house would not seem quite appropriate for me. After one has lived fifty years one has acquired a flavour [sic] that is not entirely contemporary— also one has acquired furniture with curly legs. I know some middle aged women who have ensconced themselves in "modern" houses with equally "modern" furniture replacing their old. The resulting anonymity seems to me regrettable and a little pathetic. So though I like a great many things about the newer houses— the attention given proportion and the lack of pretense—I would like a house that would seem to fit me. So there would be that for you to consider. You would be dealing with a woman who hangs pictures on her walls and rather likes eaves.[120]

In 1952, at the time of this commission, Harris, in midcareer, had recently become the dean of the School of Architecture at the University of Texas at Austin. Born in Redlands, California in 1902, Harris graduated from San

Bernardino High School moving to the Los Angeles area to attend Pomona College. He left school in his sophomore year due to ill health and upon recovering began attending the Otis Art Institute where he found himself drawn to sculpture and modeling. In 1925 he began to study drawing and painting with Stanton Macdonald-Wright at the Art Students League in Los Angeles. Macdonald-Wright's teachings on color remained a part of Harris' designs throughout his life. Inspired by a visit to Frank Lloyd Wright's Hollyhock House, Harris began to study Wright's designs and take an avid interest in the few modern buildings being erected in Los Angeles. This led him to visit the home shared by architects Richard Neutra and R. M. Schindler where he was invited to join their growing office as a draftsman. During this time he took architectural drawing classes and attended classes given by Neutra at the Los Angeles Academy of Modern Art. In 1933, he left Neutra's office to establish an independent practice in Los Angeles. His work reflected the early influences of both Wright's interest in nature and Neutra's interest in the machine. According to his biographer Lisa Germany, Harris was an early proponent and practitioner of a humane modernism that was particularly welcomed in the Bay Area.[121]

His first commissions were small homes, which he designed using modular planning for economy. His own 1935 house in Fellowship Park in Los Angeles won the 1936 *House Beautiful* Small House Competition and established his reputation in California as well as nationally.

Well-known and admired as a practitioner of modern design in the United States, Harris's style began to reflect his wife's, writer Jean Murray Bangs', advocacy of the craftsman-style architecture of Bernard Maybeck and the firm of Greene & Greene.[122] But it was "regionalism [that] had allowed Harris to unite his two great passions—California and Modern architecture —and he had done so in a convincing, even-handed way."[123] He left California in 1951 to become the head of the newly formed architecture program at the University of Texas. His new responsibilities there and lack of a license to practice architecture in California —he had let it lapse—limited his involvement in the Duhring project to "design and supervision of construction."[124] By September, Hervey Parke Clark, of the San Francisco firm Clark & Beuttler, had become the project's supervising architect.

Harris's design engages equally both the outside world and the needs of the client. The siting of the house takes advantage of views of the bay and Marin County's Mount Tamalpais to the northwest and San Francisco to the southwest. The corner windows in the living and dining rooms frame the scenery with views divided by a solid west wall. Leaving the west wall without openings may reflect a lesson learned from the unrelenting solar penetration through the glazed west face of Harris's Havens house nearby. It might also have been intended to force occupants to peer around this wall for premium views. In addition, Mrs. Duhring wanted the house to protect the privacy of their neighbor's garden.[125] In a site plan similar to the one he used for Havens, the garage announces the residence on the street before the visitor passes through a gate and between walls to reach the front door.

[4-2]
**HARWELL HAMILTON HARRIS,
HAVENS RESIDENCE, BERKELEY,
1941.**
[MAYNARD PARKER; EDA, UCB]

At the middle stages of the project, Clark wrote to Harris that the working drawings were well along but that there was concern that the garage encroached on the neighbors' property line. He also requested outline specifications, particularly concerning interior finishes, as well as a set of drawings for a comparable house to better understand Harris's intentions, particularly in terms of the details and the preferred system of modular dimensioning. Harris had experimented with numerous modular options and sizes during this period and chose to use a three-foot module as the basis for this project [figure 4-3]. Clark closed the letter by expressing the firm's enjoyment working on the project and hoped their interpretation wouldn't "fall too far short of the way you would do it yourself."[126]

Harris's distance from the project has left us a wealth of correspondence that offers unusual insight into the project's design and construction process and the cooperative nature of the architects' relationship. Clark sent detailed letters to Harris who would indicate his reactions and decisions in the right-hand margin, then send them back. For example, a September 1953 letter, "for the wood fence or garden wall, Bob [Lym, on-site project architect for Clark & Buettler] understands you wish vertical boards. Should they be butted (with or without battens) or ship lap?" Harris wrote in the margin that his preference would be "with battens." The same letter included Harris's choice of firebrick for the mantel, oak for the stairs and upper floors, ponderosa pine for the trim, doors, and sashes, and putty for glazing, as it "proves more water tight in Berkeley."[127]

By mid-October, Mrs. Duhring had begun her requests for design changes. She regretted that the original plan had included only one bathroom on the main floor, and based on the advice of several friends, she now wished to incorporate a second one into the design (she didn't get one). The detail contained in her letters may have provided more information than required at the time but seen from the distance of half a century, they have a certain historical charm. Duhring informed Harris that while one friend felt a second bathroom increased the house's future "salability," another felt it was nice to "keep the sheep from the goats in case of a party."[128] This long letter described in detail, and in sketches, bathroom mirrors, floor and counter surfaces, and kitchen appliances. In response to his query about the garbage grinder she wrote: "Personally I feel some plan for an incinerator would be more vital—papers have seemed more of a problem than grapefruit rinds to me."

Now that she had become involved in building her own house, Duhring noticed all sorts of desirable features in other people's homes and was continually running these possibilities by Harris. Some of her thoughts included: not using shingles, finding houses with horizontal redwood boards attractive, and possibly preferring rooms with wood rather than plaster walls. She finally admitted that she was concerned about his designing her home from Texas and wrote that "it is going to be rather hard on you being at a distance. Were you at the other end of a telephone you could know when I had a new idea when it was very young and nebulous and could either approve or nip it in the bud as seemed advisable.

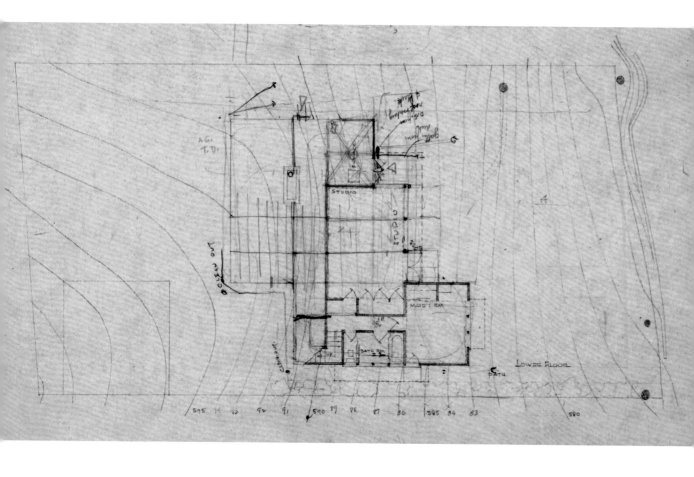

[4-3]
**DUHRING RESIDENCE,
MAIN FLOOR STUDY.**

[ALEXANDER ARCHITECTURAL
ARCHIVE, UNIVERSITY OF TEXAS,
AUSTIN, HEREAFTER AA, UTA]

Now when I have to write a letter the idea has gotten quite a sturdy growth before you hear of it—like the bathrooms for instance."[129]

By November Mrs. Duhring was asking Harris to "make up my mind for me a little about the shingles—I do want a new look."[130] Clark wrote Harris noting that the drawings and specifications were complete—with the exception of the garage—and explained that he had refrained from contacting Mrs. Duhring himself, believing that all contact should be through Harris until he approved the work. Clark inquired whether Harris would like the office to review the drawings with her directly and requested the names of any contractors Harris wanted included as bidders. Harris replied to both Clark and Duhring, indicating he would review the drawings during the Thanksgiving holiday.

In December 1953, Harris wrote to Wurster with questions about the architecture curriculum at Berkeley. Responding to the questions, Wurster added that "Greenwood Common continues to be interesting and I am eager to see what you will come up with for Ruth Duhring."[131] He sympathized that scheduling and/or distance seemed to slow down work. And indeed, after the New Year a slow period evolved as Clark awaited Harris's response to the drawings, but in February things picked up. Clark sent further lists of questions and received Harris's responses to them, although Harris did not respond to the repeated inquiry about contractors. Bob Lym finally began meeting with Mrs. Duhring to review the plans at which time she expressed her concerns about flooring and a freestanding fireplace for the lower level.

With the approval of the specifications in March 1954, the process of selecting a contractor began. For Mrs. Duhring, the receipt of the plans and specifications unleashed a spate of letters requesting Harris's approval for a number of things she would like changed, such as enlarging the dining room and making the kitchen smaller, as well as including a built-in chest to take the place of a bureau in a bedroom. Her concern was that "so often built in drawers look institutional or like a fraternity house, but if you yourself designed it, it would be all right and might perhaps make the room look better than a bureau sitting in that little cove."[132]

In May, Mrs. Duhring continued to share her concerns about the living room fireplace. She reminded Harris that "when we first talked about the fireplace it was not all brick as it is now and I imagine you can envision the end of the room with the brick being better —But would it spoil your place if we had a wooden shelf? I like wood—it seems gentler than brick—pleasanter to the touch—a dust cloth doesn't rasp over it—it would perhaps be more even." She also reminded him that she would still like to have two bathrooms on the main floor where he has only one in the plan.[133]

Clark wrote to Harris in mid-July informing him that the framing was about to begin and that he required a response about the mantle in the living room, the flooring, and the built-in cabinets on the lower floor. He also requested Harris's opinion on Mrs. Duhring's idea for a bench on the deck, "which she believes would be more useful than putting out chairs."[134] Clark's letter crossed one from Harris in the mail. In it he informed both Clark and Duhring that he was planning an August visit to Berkeley to make decisions on the color of finishes, design of the garden, and other matters—nonetheless, he immediately wrote back to resolve the issues raised in Clark's letter.

From the west the house appears as a series of pitched-roof cottages. Harris used similar overlapping peaks in his 1951 Chadwick School in Rolling Hills, California. These express the three distinct sections of the main house, each having either access to a deck or a view of the bay. The west slope of the garage roof shelters the walk that leads to the entry garden and front door [figure 4-4]. The extended roofline is perhaps the design's most interesting feature, particularly where the ridge of the main section overlaps that of the bedrooms. Both walls and roofs were clad in red cedar shingles in keeping with the design guidelines preferred by the residents of the Common. The square-cut beam ends serve as ornamental details that elegantly terminate the plane of the roof.

Facing the Common, the south elevation façade appears as a long, one-story unit. Its three divisions reflect the interior uses behind them. An outdoor room mirrors each interior space along the south elevation: entrance hall, kitchen, and dining room, each has an echoing outdoor room. Three-dimensional elements along the north elevation reveal distinct functional spaces—master bedroom with protruding balcony and living room with wraparound deck. Like the other three houses on the north side of the Common, this one also has a lower level in response to the slope to Rose Street [figure 4-5]. Unlike the other residences in the enclave, the Duhring house was

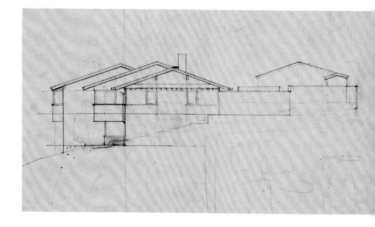

[4-4]
DUHRING RESIDENCE,
WEST ELEVATION, c. 1954.
[AA, UTA]

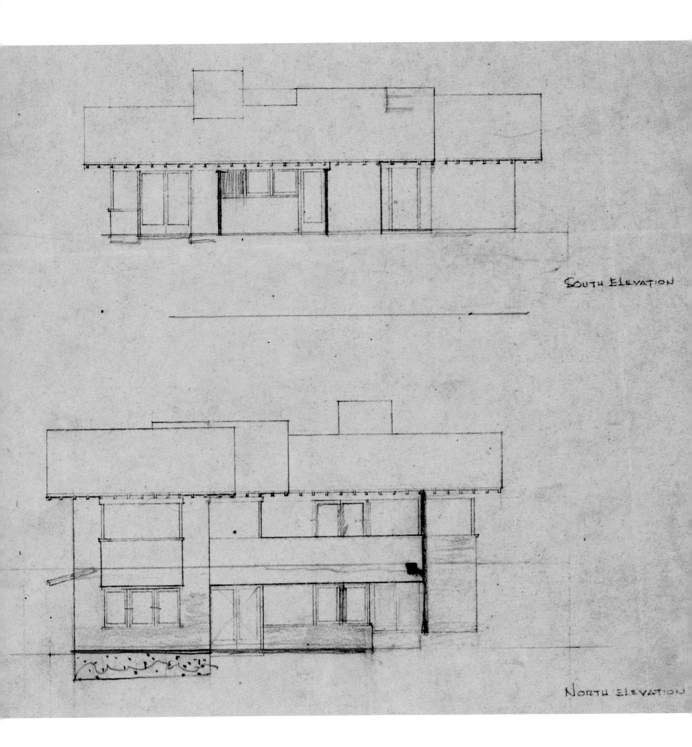

SOUTH ELEVATION

NORTH ELEVATION

[4-5]
**DUHRING RESIDENCE, SOUTH
AND NORTH ELEVATIONS, c. 1954.**
[AA, UTA]

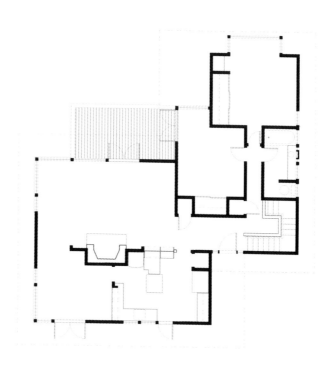

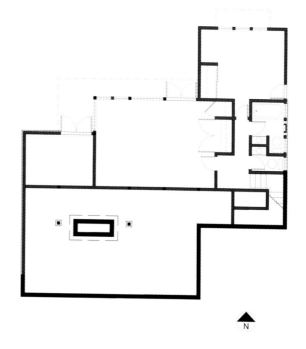

[4-6A]
**DUHRING RESIDENCE,
MAIN FLOOR PLAN.**
[MATTHEW GUËREÑA, 2008]

[4-6B]
**DUHRING RESIDENCE,
LOWER FLOOR PLAN.**
[MATTHEW GUËREÑA, 2008]

N

built partway down the slope to Rose Street, not on grade with the Common. Approached by a short flight of stairs, the house appears nestled in the slope with the garden as a buffer between public and private terrain.

The plan of the Duhring house illustrates a number of entries on Harris's list of nine do's and don'ts for the small house published in *California Arts & Architecture* in 1935. These included directives such as:

Don't make rooms serve as halls...

Accept the fact that light attracts, and give every room a sunny exposure.

Deserted space is wasted space.

Plan the walls of a room in scale with its floor: That is, in a small or narrow room reduce the height of the openings and lower the ceiling.

Plan the building not as a hollow box cut up into cells, but as a series of partially enclosed spaces opening into one another. By partial screening create the feeling of space beyond.[135]

As completed, the living room, dining room, and two bedrooms are all located on the entry level, and all but the master bedroom have an open view to the west [figures 4-6A, 4-6B]. The living room is set on the north side of the house. Its deck overhangs the steep drop to Rose Street and has an excellent view of the 1912 Howard residence below to the west. Like the Havens house, Harris complemented most of the main spaces with glazed walls and exterior decks. In contrast, however, the internal spaces of the Duhring house appear less integrated and more distinct. While this separation reflects, in

[4-7]
**DUHRING RESIDENCE, LIVING
ROOM LOOKING SOUTHWEST.**
[MARC TREIB]

part, the client's desires, it may also indicate Harris's transition from a strict modern vocabulary to a softer style influenced by his increasing involvement with Arts-and-Crafts historicism.[136]

Throughout the house, Harris paid careful attention to the lighting. Interior lamps are installed either in the soffits with diffusing panels or as upward-facing fluorescent tubes. All the windows are square following the three-foot grid used throughout the house. A brick fireplace in the middle of the house contributes to the separation of the living and dining rooms [figure 4-7]. Harris used rectangular "baffles" in the east and west corners of the living room ceiling above the fireplace to create an axis parallel to the roofline—and to create a lower ceiling height in scale with dimensions of the room. The lower floor includes a studio for Mrs. Duhring, a maid's room, and a second bathroom. The studio, as well as the living and dining rooms, has French doors that open onto outdoor space, whether patio, deck, or garden. Harris enjoyed the use of strong colors, and his client assured him that she approved his choices of light yellow, blue, and coral as the main hues.

The garage, a separate structure facing the access road, had always been problematic. From the very beginning difficulties had plagued decisions about the garage's location in relation to the easement, difficulties discussed in numerous letters throughout the project. Over time it became a contentious issue even between Harris and Wurster, who wrote to Harris in July 1954 asking him "to forgive my frankness in writing how heartsick several of us are at the insistence and height of the Duhring garage.

Were you here, with your sensitivity, it could never have happened." He explained that it blocked the view from several houses and the sun from the Duhring and Ackerman homes, writing that this is "possibly the reason I do doubt absentee designers for if you were here it would have been down before this."[137]

Despite Wurster's intent to remain detached from design issues related to the Common, he was drawn into the garage imbroglio. He bemoaned the situation in a September letter to architect and friend O'Neil Ford, writing that Harris was designing the Duhring house and that it was "delightful and beautiful when suddenly the garage sprang up which is needlessly high and deprives one neighbor of sun, several of view." One Common owner phoned him to request that he do something, as they assumed he had the privilege of providing some thoughts on the situation, but, as Wurster wrote, despite feeling he knew Harris well enough, Harris had ignored his letter and "not only did he [Harris] have the discourtesy not to answer it but came up here, looked at the building, told a neighbor it was just what he expected and wanted, and departed—not even having the generosity to call me." Wurster went on to express his distress, asking Ford, "what does one do about such [a] needless will to hurt ... I feel strongly about architects who place abstract design above human values of neighbors."[138]

The correspondence indicates that part of the problem may have lain with the process of construction. Mrs. Duhring contacted Harris to complain about the builder who had been ignoring her. She wrote that the "garage is a case in point. As soon as I saw the frame I asked him to wait till you had seen it. The next day he put on the sheet rock. Again I asked him to stop and the next I know it was partially shingled. Had he waited when first spoken to it could have been lowered at less expense than now goes into additional fences—or if your decision had been to go on as it was, at least the neighbors would have been placated by knowing they had been considered."[139]

Harris's distance, the client's temperament, and the number of parties involved rendered this a complex and, at times, difficult project. In April 1956, the final punch list was submitted to the contractor as was a letter from Harris to Clark in which he apologized for his having had so much trouble with the Duhring job and he expressed his appreciation for all Clark had done.[140] Problems with the contractor led to an exchange of letters as late as 1957 among Harris, Duhring, and Clark; final payment was finally acknowledged by Clark in June 1958. As Clarke wrote to Harris, "Generally the work proved a great deal more demanding than we had anticipated, particularly in the end dealing with the contractor."[141]

Subsequent owners of the Duhring house included Woodbridge Bingham, a professor of Chinese studies and East Asian history, and his wife, Ursula, a founding member of the Women's Town Council of Berkeley. They were succeeded by the current owners, who have restored the original colors and maintained the original footprint and what they feel is the original idea behind the house—despite a number of interior changes required by a growing family with children. These changes included removing the fireplace mantel and a 1988 kitchen remodeling that enlarged the kitchen and increased its access to the dining room. Additional changes to the lower level included adding a master bedroom, a new access door, and converting a utility space into a small bedroom.[142]

The garden's fences and gates were essential elements of the design.[143] Harris's original scheme included an entrance garden reached by descending a brick path and stairs. The fence screened one side of a service yard entered from either the path or the kitchen. A fence to the west sets off a paved patio and a garden by Geraldine Knight Scott accessible from the dining room. The plan reflects one of Harris' nine directions for potential homebuilders:

Make one whole wall of the room of glass and open the room into a garden. With the solid material that the glass replaced, build a wall around the garden. Place the floor of the garden next to the glass, making the outer floor only an inch or two lower than the inner floor. The garden then becomes the outer portion of the room, separated from the inner portion by a removable glass screen.[144]

In an undated letter, probably from summer 1954, Mrs. Duhring informed Harris that after giving the matter a great deal of thought, she was going to have Mrs. Scott take over the landscape design. She assured Harris that were he there she would naturally turn to him for all the small but important details.[145] Scott began designing the gardens shortly thereafter [figure 4-8].

[4-8]
**GERALDINE KNIGHT SCOTT,
DUHRING GARDEN, PLAN, 1957.**
[EDA, UCB]

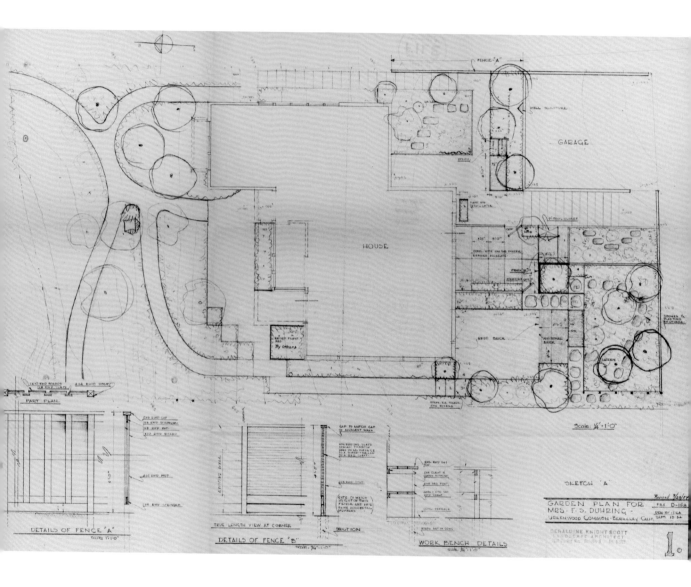

PART PLAN

DETAILS OF FENCE "A"
Scale: 1"=1'-0"

TRUE LENGTH VIEW AT CORNER

SECTION

DETAILS OF FENCE "B"
Scale: 3/4"=1'-0"

WORK BENCH DETAILS
Scale: 3/4"=1'-0"

HOUSE

GARAGE

WALL SCULPTURE

Scale: 1/4"=1'-0"

SKETCH "A"

Revised 1/23/44

GARDEN PLAN FOR
MRS. F. S. DUHRING.
GREENWOOD COMMON - BERKELEY, CALIF.

FILE D-168

GERALDINE KNIGHT SCOTT
LANDSCAPE ARCHITECT

1.

[4-9]
**GERALDINE KNIGHT SCOTT,
DUHRING GARDEN.**
THE SOUTH GARDEN FACES
THE DINING ROOM.
[MARC TREIB]

Geraldine Knight Scott received her degree in landscape architecture from the University of California, Berkeley, College of Agriculture in 1926 and continued her education in art and architecture at Cornell University (1926–1928). Following graduation she was employed in the southern California office of A. E. Hanson, working on various projects that included the Harold Lloyd estate in Beverly Hills. Beginning in 1930 Scott spent twenty-two months in Europe surveying historic Italian villas, exploring the gardens of France and Spain, and attending the Sorbonne in Paris. Returning to California in 1933, she joined the office of Helen Van Pelt in Marin County and worked on the "Pacific Area" of the Pacific House at the 1939 Golden Gate International Exposition. That same year she married Mellier Scott, a Los Angeles journalist who would later become a noted authority in city and regional planning. They moved to Berkeley in 1941 and in 1948 she began her twenty-year private practice, during which she also taught landscape architecture at the University of California.[146]

In a September 1954 plan Scott added to the small brick patio outside the dining room and proposed a Japanese-style design for the entrance garden that combined stepping-stones with flowering trees and shrubs [figure 4-9]. Working around existing concrete pavers and natural stones she added a lantern and wall sculpture on the rear wall of the garage that faced the front door of the house. The following spring she specified plants and designed additional fencing and a front gate.[147] Her proposed planting scheme included nine species of trees and shrubs—mostly flowering varieties—including Japanese maple (*Acer palmatum*), fuchsia, rhododendron, flowering crabapple, dogwood, cherry, and magnolia. She also placed a jacaranda in the center of the front garden. This was a garden intended to bloom profusely, with twenty-seven kinds of shrubs, many of them flowering varieties, roses, and clematis and other kinds of flowering vines. Surrounding these plants, and interspersed with the hardscape, were twenty-five kinds of groundcovers and perennials. It was a garden scheme rich in species that relied on planting to work its magic.

The Duhring house enfolds two generations of regional design, blending the look, feel, and scale of a Craftsman home with midcentury modern spaces and materials. The result is a cozy and charming house nestled on its hillside, an architectural citizen contributing quietly to the community of Greenwood Common.

Baer Residence

7 Greenwood Common

Clients:

A. Sasha Kaun (1940– c. 1950)

William and Catherine Wurster, (1951–1953)

Mr. &. Mrs. Morley Baer (1953–1972)

Architects:

Rudolph Schindler, 1940 (remodel for Kaun)

William W. Wurster, c. 1952 (alterations)

Henry Hill, c. 1953–54 (remodel for Baer)

Landscape Architect:
Lawrence Halprin, 1955

Number 7 Greenwood Common (originally 1431 Le Roy Avenue) presents the most complicated history of residents and remodels of all the homes on the Common [figure 5-1]. Local lore reports a building on the site from the 1920s, a structure believed to be the Gregory's guest house. A small house appears on the Sanborn Fire Insurance map of 1911 and a larger one on the 1929 map, suggesting that additions or other modifications may have been made during the intervening years [see figure 5-4]. In 1940 the Austrian émigré architect Rudolph Schindler altered this structure for A. Sasha Kaun, the last of his three renovation projects in the Berkeley Hills [figures 5-2, 5-3].[148]

Soon after returning to Berkeley from Cambridge in 1950, the Wursters—Bill, Catherine, and their young daughter Sadie—rented a house on Buena Vista Way, quite close to the site that would become Greenwood Common. They didn't stay there long, however, moving into Schindler's Kaun house, intending to sell it when Wurster's project for Greenwood Common materialized. In 1951, during the process of creating Greenwood Common, Wurster wrote to Douglas Haskell, "We have bought 'Termite Villa' next to the lot we hope to own and will do some work on it to move in on 1 July." And just a month later, on April 14, he wrote to Harry Bent, "We have just bought a terrible house—6 rooms on 5 levels designed by Schindler—over the telephone from some mad Russians. But it has a superb location and a superb 360 degree view."[149]

Wurster led the negotiations to establish Greenwood Common as both a residential development and a corporation. Once the lots were registered, the property transferred, and

[5-1]
R. M. SCHINDLER, 1940;
WILLIAM WURSTER, c. 1952;
HENRY HILL, c.1954;
BAER RESIDENCE,
GREENWOOD COMMON, BERKELEY.
LOOKING NORTH FROM
THE COMMON.
[MARC TREIB]

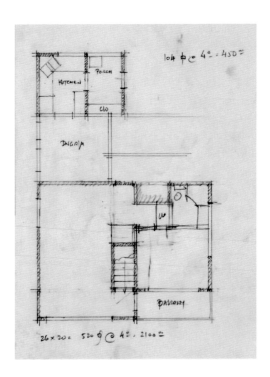

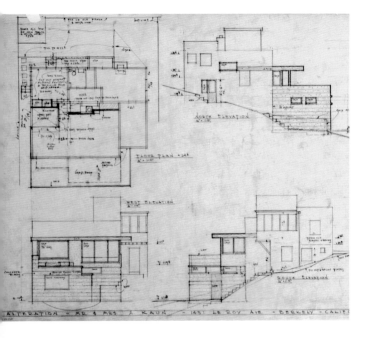

the corporation a going concern, he clarified how his property would relate to the Common. In a September 22, 1952, memo he explained that he owned two lots: one, a forty-one-foot-wide lot on Le Roy Avenue with three small dwellings, and what became the undersized lot 7 on Greenwood Common. He chose to sever the lower portion of the lot facing Le Roy and join the upper portion to lot 7 [see figure B-10].

This change would augment the size of lot 7, putting it on equal footing with the other properties and removing any confusion that the two lower cottages were part of the Common. He also revealed that he was considering purchasing the large Gregory house to the east of the Common and was thus giving owners or their friends the first opportunity to purchase lot 7.[150] It was at this time that Wurster undertook some minor remodeling of the house by closing off the front door that faced Le Roy Avenue, and repositioning it on the northeast corner of the house, thereby reorienting the entrance toward the Common.

Following their 1953 move into the old Gregory house the Wursters sold lot 7 to architectural photographer Morley Baer and his wife Frances, also a photographer.[151] Baer had photographed several Wurster projects, and Wurster later designed a house for him on the Big Sur coast near Carmel. Baer had also photographed projects for architect Henry Hill, and the Baers soon hired Hill to design improvements and additions to the Schindler/Wurster House that had become 7 Greenwood Common [figure 5-4].

Born in 1913, Henry Hill had studied architecture at the University of California, Berkeley (B. Arch, 1936), and at Harvard's Graduate

School of Design (M. Arch, 1938), where he studied under Walter Gropius. Returning to the Bay Area, he joined the office of John Elkin Dinwiddie in San Francisco and became a partner in 1939. Following wartime service in the U.S. Army Corps of Engineers, Hill rejoined Dinwiddie and his new partner Erich Mendelsohn, a well-known émigré German architect, to form the firm of Dinwiddie, Mendelsohn & Hill. Dinwiddie left the partnership soon after and Hill and Mendelsohn worked together from 1945 to 1947. Their projects included two residences in Berkeley and designs for a synagogue in St. Louis.

In 1948 Hill opened his own practice and designed residences throughout the Bay Area, in Carmel, southern California, Illinois, Connecticut, and Kentucky. Like other Greenwood architects, Hill combined international modernism with regional and vernacular influences and materials, spicing them with his appreciation of color and light. Given his frequent use and thus association with wood, his versatility was demonstrated when he consulted with the U.S. Steel Corporation in the design of a prototype steel house. It is clear from Wurster's correspondence that he had been friendly with Hill for some time prior to the development of Greenwood Common. Hill's sponsors for his 1953 membership application for the Northern California Chapter of the AIA were Wurster partners Donn Emmons and Theodore Bernardi, each of whom stated that they had known Hill for twelve years. Wurster's own appreciation of Hill's work was expressed in a letter describing the Common to Buckminster Fuller in which he declared that Morley Baer and his wife bought the house and Henry Hill did a wonderful job of remodeling it.[152]

[5-4]
R.M. SCHINDLER, ALTERATIONS FOR MR. & MRS. A. KAUN.
VIEW FROM COMMON, c. 1953.
[AA, UP]

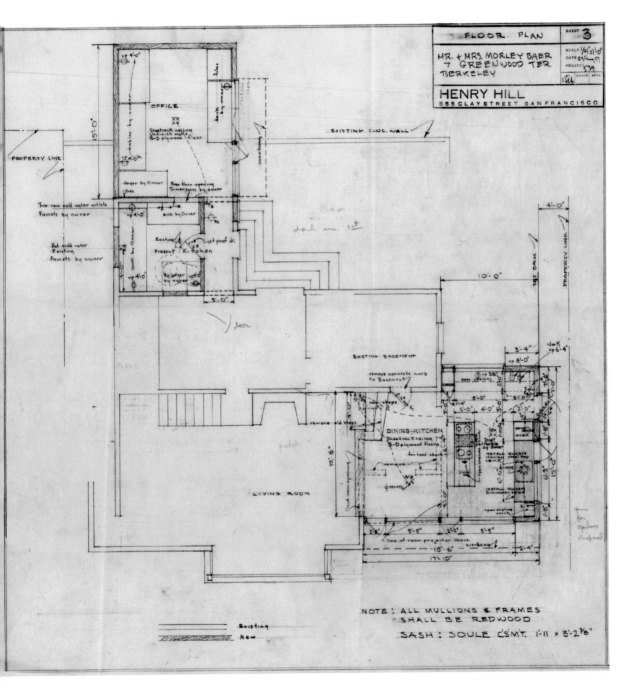

FLOOR PLAN SHEET 3

MR. + MRS. MORLEY BAER
7 GREENWOOD TER.
BERKELEY

SCALE 1/4"=1'-0"
DATE 23 June 59
PROJECT 539
CHECK. APPD.

HENRY HILL
555 CLAY STREET SAN FRANCISCO

OFFICE

Sheetrock ceiling
Unfinish walls
3-D plywood floor

EXISTING CONC. WALL

PROPERTY LINE

dryer by Owner
gas

Pass thru opening
Dimensions by owner

Two new cold water outlets
Faucets by owner

sink by Owner

Existing
Present Kitchen

light proof dr.

Hot cold water
Existing
Faucets by owner

dark rm. 1st

PROPERTY LINE

4'-0"

10'-0"

EXISTING BASEMENT

remove concrete curb
to Basement

remove old steps

new steps

DINING-KITCHEN
Sheet rock Ceiling
3-D plywood floors

OVEN

LIVING ROOM

line of room projection above.

15'-6"
17'-10"

Existing

New

NOTE: ALL MULLIONS & FRAMES
SHALL BE REDWOOD

SASH: SOULE CSMT. 1'-11 x 3'-2 3/8"

In a 1961 presentation entitled "Confusion in Architecture" Hill expressed his design philosophy by averring that "our fundamentals are so simple: orientation, use, circulation, proportion, and scale. We must express them with thought and with sensitivity: then we shall have an ordered architecture…and not the order of cold precision, but the order of knowledge. Above all, we have an understanding of the human individual."[153] Both of his projects at Greenwood Common illustrate this understanding.

The site for what became lot 7, originally oriented to Le Roy Avenue, drops steeply on three sides. This challenging topography, combined with reorienting the house to face the Common, resulted in significant remodeling on the east side. In fact, the first modifications for the Baers included replacing the existing kitchen with a large darkroom and creating an office facing the Common on the same level as the sitting room [figure 5-5]. To include their business office and darkroom within the residence the Baers were required to obtain a special use permit. In order to receive the permit they had to stipulate that as architectural photographers, who did most of their work offsite, there would be no home studio and there would be no retail business at that address. They assured the Berkeley authorities that all photographs would be mailed and only photographs taken by the Baers would be handled. In addition, there were to be no employees (this was modified in 1959 to allow a bookkeeper-secretary), structures would have a residential exterior without signs or nameplates, and developing equipment would not interfere with other electrical services, radios, or televisions

nearby. The Baers had the freestanding carport adjacent to the front door designed to be clearly recognizable so that guests would not approach the office door in error [figures 5-6, 5-7].

Despite being pieced together and dispersed on three levels, the house has a wonderfully coherent feel. The entrance enfolds a small foyer added in 1984 to replace the doorway that Wurster had added.[154] It leads to the living room and accesses a flight of stairs to the second story. The living room, one of the original Schindler spaces, is filled with light reflected from the white walls and energized by the magnificent view through the wall of windows that overlook the bay [figure 5-8]. The walls, originally wood, were painted white in the mid-1970s, "it took about ten coats of paint to cover the seven kinds of wood paneling in the living room."[155] The fireplace opposes the wall of windows.

The second floor features a small but comfortable sitting room graced by a view of the Halprin-designed garden through glass doors on its east side. In 1961, a third-story, built over the darkroom and containing a bedroom and bath, was added for the Baer's son, Joshua. Most of the rooms designed by Schindler are, by more recent standards, quite small. It is therefore not surprising that following their move to the Gregory house, Wurster wrote to Alvar Aalto of this sudden contrast in living conditions: "We live in a marvelous old barn of a house—Florence Knoll says it is straight out of Finland—with great pines all around it" and to other correspondents that their new living room was large enough for Sadie to turn cartwheels.[156]

[5-5]
HENRY HILL, BAER RESIDENCE,
FLOOR PLAN, 1953.
[EDA, UCB]

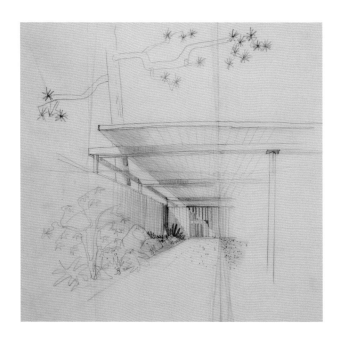

[5-6]
**LAWRENCE HALPRIN,
BAER RESIDENCE,
ENTRANCE STUDY, c. 1954.**
〔EDA, UCB〕

[5-7]
**LAWRENCE HALPRIN,
BAER RESIDENCE,
ENTRANCE AND CARPORT.**

〔MORLEY BAER; EDA, UCB〕

Although it is difficult to identify Schindler's efforts buried within the existing building, remnants of the original structure and spaces survive on both the interior and exterior. However, it is the architectural and landscape additions on the east side of the house—for example, the carport and enclosed garden—that most conclusively transformed the site. The landscape, including decks, patios, and plantings, was designed by Lawrence Halprin who knew Baer through his work as an architectural photographer.[157] This project, like Halprin's gardens for the Maenchens, illustrates the intricate working relationship between client and designer. In this case there was a professional relationship as well: Halprin was paid in part by exchanging services with Baer. In a fall 1954 letter to Halprin, the Baers included a plot plan, snapshots, and thoughts on the work to be done, assuring Halprin that the items listed were not meant to limit his imagination.[158]

Listed were general aspects of the work as well as specific ideas for the garden, carport, entry, and fences—all reflected the Baers' personality. For example, in his notes Morley remarked that "if we have one concern about a landscape designer it is that he will design the hell out of the place. The less design that shows the better."[159] They requested privacy for sunbathing, flexibility of use, protection from the wind whipping up the hill from the southwest, and complete enclosure for child safety. Suggestions listed for the garden were fairly specific:

> - Great Flexibility, a non-designed look like the little garden across the street
> - White blooms, we love em [sic]
> - Begonias, we got em, still in Carmel.

[5-8]
BAER RESIDENCE, LIVING ROOM.
[MARC TREIB]

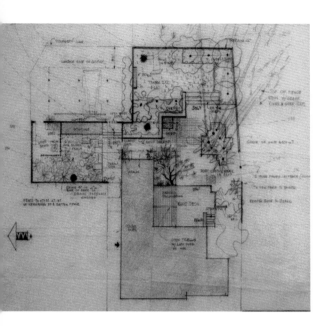

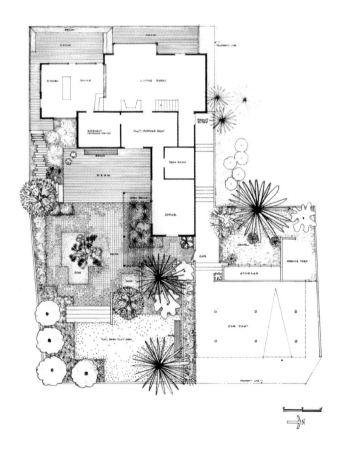

[5-9]
**LAWRENCE HALPRIN,
BAER GARDEN, PRELIMINARY
PLAN, 1954.**

[AA, UP]

[5-10]
**BAER GARDEN, GARDEN PLAN,
1955.**

NOTE: THE ORIENTATIONS OF THE
TWO PLANS ARE REVERSED.

[AA, UP]

112

- Beach stones, we can get em.
*- [We] Like fruit trees. Also birch, aspen,
maple (maybe on windy corner?)*
*- Fatsehedera—as ground cover around
other plants*
*- Brick—or preferable wood blocks, if we
can make a deal involving photographs
with one of the manufacturers*
*- Benches, wide and handsome. One
with some storage space beneath.*
*- Must keep the wild rose that is seen
from east window wall of kitchen.*
- Sand box area—small—for Josho.
*- Small potting counter, three small bins
underneath counter.*[160]

Halprin's initial sketch captured the desires of the clients, and the final design displayed few changes from it: only the orientation of the carport changed by ninety degrees and less planting was proposed for the play area [figure 5-9].

Construction of this outdoor living area began in 1955 with the addition of wood decks along both the south and west sides of the house. Some residents of the Common objected to the south deck, concerned that sunshades or awnings added to the deck would constitute unwarranted construction on the property— although the deck itself, set just below the brow of the hill, would not be visible. There was also concern that the west deck might overhang the hill, providing a view that compromised the privacy of the cottages on Le Roy. To address these concerns, the Baers guaranteed that there would be no structures added to shade the deck.

The fenced garden exceeded the footprint of the house, providing nearly as many "rooms" outside as within [figure 5-10]. The first of these rooms was a wooden deck that led to a generous brick patio, whose focal point was a sculptural pine tree surrounded by large rocks [figure 5-11]. This patio met the office wing under a wisteria-covered trellis and extended in front of the office to the entryway to the north. For their son, a small sandbox was tucked into the north-east corner of the brick patio. A flight of four steps led to a tanbark play area with a "jungle jim" that afforded a view above the fence to the Common beyond [figure 5-12].

In response to the Baer's suggestions, a white wisteria climbed the trellis along the office wall, complementing white plantings such as of agapanthus, *Campanula isophylla* 'Alba' and *Magnolia stellata* 'Waterlily' [figure 5-13]. Low trees were planted in the small spaces to the east of the sandbox and along the southeast corner of the play area. An additional bed encircled an existing pine tree near the carport. An article published in *Progressive Architecture* in 1961, with photographs by Baer and text by Halprin, explained that the carport was intended both to shelter cars and serve as a gateway to the house and as a spatial transition from the openness of the Common.[161]

Pieced together over time by numerous owners and designers, the house is extremely livable and the spaces well integrated. The changing uses of rooms on the second and third levels attest to the flexibility of the design, and their verticality is balanced by the horizontal, divided spaces of the garden [figure 5-14].

[5-11]
LAWRENCE HALPRIN,
BAER GARDEN, LOOKING EAST
TOWARD GREENWOOD COMMON.

[MORLEY BAER, AA, UP; c. 1963,]

[5-12]
**BAER GARDEN, PLAY AREA
WITH GREENWOOD COMMON
IN BACKGROUND.**
[MORLEY BAER, AA, UP; c. 1955]

[5-13]
**BAER GARDEN, WHITE WISTERIA
OUTSIDE OFFICE.**
[MORLEY BAER, AA, UP; c. 1963]

[5-14] *overleaf*
BAER HOUSE AND GARDEN.
[CRIS BENTON, 2008]

118

Douglas Residence

8 Greenwood Common, 1953

Client:
Mrs. W. W. (Helen Cooper) Douglas

Architect:
Howard Moïse

Garden Designer:
Howard Moïse

In 1952, at the time of the establishment of the Common, Mrs. Douglas, an antique collector, lived close by at 1409 Greenwood Terrace. How she came to commission Howard Moïse to design her home and how the design progressed are not known. We do know, however, that she signed construction drawings some time before October 1952 [figure 6-1].

Perhaps it was Wurster, with whom Moïse taught, who recommended him to Mrs. Douglas. Moïse, considerably older than the other architects designing houses for the Common, was born in New Mexico in 1887, earning both his bachelor's degree (1915) and Masters of Architecture (1916) at Harvard University. Unlike most of the other architects of residences on the Common Moïse served in World War I rather than in World War II. Prior to receiving an offer of a professorship in Berkeley's School of Architecture in 1932 he had being working in the New York office of James Gamble Rogers, where he was responsible for the design of the façade of the Columbia Presbyterian Medical Center complex and for planning and designing several elements of the group.

A compact single-story house on the southeast corner of the Common, the Douglas house packs a number of small private rooms into the north part of the building. Essentially, it turns its back on the Common to create an outdoor environment of its own facing the Berkeley Hills. A short walkway, shared with lot 9, connects the allée of flowering plum trees with the Douglas's front door. The living room with its mammoth fireplace, lofty ceiling, and exposed rafters gives the house the feel of a mountain cabin. The house shares similar materials and design elements with the other

[6-1]
HOWARD MOÏSE, DOUGLAS RESIDENCE, GREENWOOD COMMON, BERKELEY, 1953.
SEEN FROM THE EAST SHORTLY AFTER OCCUPANCY.
[EDA, UCB]

houses on the Common: the flow of the living and dining rooms onto the patio through glass floor-to-ceiling doors. But its proportions, spatial relationships, and detailing make the building feel oddly different and the least "modern" of all the residences in the enclave. The house for Mrs. Douglas exhibits strong elements of earlier residences designed by Moïse [figures 6-2, 6-3].

The living quarters form the long leg of the L, while the carport and storage closets are tucked into the short leg. Given that the Common is to the north and the most spectacular views are to the west, the decision to orient the house to face the hills eastward was most likely determined by the site: the flat terrain offered no view to the Golden Gate and proximity to the house next door threatened its privacy. Perhaps it was the desire for privacy that led to placing the carport between the patio and the Common, rather than having the patio adjacent to the main entrance. An early sketch for the east elevation shows a fence separating an unenclosed patio from the carport, but later studies show that this patio was soon fenced. A chimney on the north side of the house balanced that on the south, but it served only mechanical purposes and was not connected to a second fireplace [figure 6-4].

Mrs. Douglas wanted a modern, functional home that would harmonize with her collection of antique furniture. The living room fills the south side of the plan with the fully glazed east wall reflecting the full wall of bookcases on the west. The living room, formal dining area, and entry vestibule were partly separated by a seven-foot-high screen of redwood boards and battens. The screen was designed so that

[6-2] *above*
**HOWARD MOISE, HUFFAKER
RESIDENCE, LAFAYETTE, 1948.**
[GEORGE TAGNEY; EDA, UCB]

[6-3] *below*
**HOWARD MOISE, ANDERSON
RESIDENCE, ORINDA, 1947.**
[GEORGE TAGNEY; EDA, UCB]

[6-4]
DOUGLAS RESIDENCE,
PERSPECTIVE, 1952.
[EDA, UCB]

a portion could be folded back, out of the way, to unite the spaces. According to written reports, the ceiling boards were stained dark brown while the beams were painted a gray-pink.[162] A large fireplace of pink Roman brick with a cement hearth dominates the room, which rises nearly thirteen feet to the center of a sloping roof. The plans suggest a choice of marble or plaster for the fireplace, but marble apparently seemed inappropriately formal and was not used. A bathroom and small bedroom are set to the bay side, with the master bedroom given a view of the Common. Kitchen, utility, and mechanical rooms complete the plan on the east side [figure 6-5]. The bedroom, utility space, and carport on the north side are shaded by the Common's allée of plum trees. By today's standards the bed and bathrooms of the Douglas house are quite small, even for a single person.

The Douglas house is only one of the Common's three houses with a pitched roof. Unlike the other two, the roofline runs perpendicular to the Common rather than parallel to it. Horizontal redwood and Douglas fir boards sheath the exterior of the house affixed to the supporting frame with wide nails forming a pattern that was echoed by the Winfield Scott Wellington house across the street [figure 6-6].

The original plantings were functional as well as ornamental. To soften the impact of a fence erected for security and privacy in front of the bedroom windows, Moïse lined its inside face with a four-foot hedge that reached just below the bedroom window. The remainder of the Common side was planted with tall shrubs and bordered by a low hedge that matched the hedge wrapping the neighboring lot 9 [figure 6-7].[163] The courtyard garden was paved with square concrete units divided by redwood strips.

Nestled into the pocket created between the house and garage, the garden featured a raised circle for plantings with trees, shrubs, and flowering plants in beds and pots around the perimeter. In a 1955 letter from Lawrence Halprin to Mrs. Douglas he suggested plants she might "find rewarding," although the plan for this "outdoor area" was designed by Howard Moïse [figure 6-8].[164]

Moïse also prepared plans for an addition in 1962. It included a second-story unit facing the Common comprised of a studio with a freestanding fireplace, bathroom, and small kitchen. Mrs. Douglas was probably considering this unit as accommodations for live-in help or as a rental unit. In any event, the addition was never constructed [figure 6-9].

During the 1960s and early 1970s it was common practice throughout the Common to modify the original carports. The second owner of the Douglas house was Berkeley professor Victor Jones, a colleague of Thomas Blaisdell then living next door on lot 9. Jones received a permit to enclose part of the carport for use as a study. He explained in the permit application that as the carport already had two sides and a roof, this would not add another structure and off-street parking would be maintained. He assured the planning department that "the enclosure would be in the same style as the house and the fence as designed by the architect."[165]

This house does little to welcome the visitor despite being the first residence encountered upon entering the plum allée. The remaining carport facing Greenwood Terrace, and the high fence separating the house from the entrance path, permit no visual access or understanding of this house anchoring its corner of the Common.

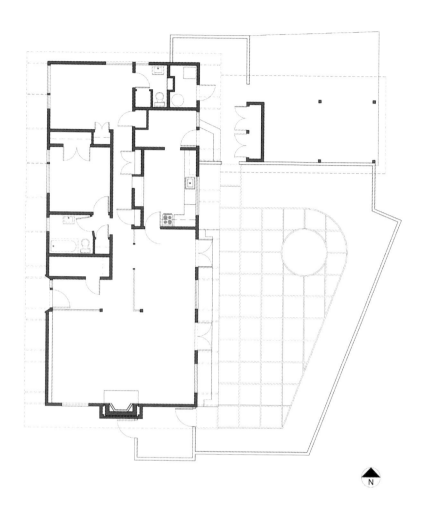

[6-5]
DOUGLAS RESIDENCE.
FLOOR PLAN.
[MATTHEW GÜËREÑA, 2008]

[6-6]
DOUGLAS RESIDENCE.
EAST FAÇADE.
[WAYNE ANDREWS; EDA, UCB]

[6-7] *opposite above*
**DOUGLAS AND BLAISDELL
RESIDENCES.**
VIEW LOOKING WEST.
[MORLEY BAER, UCSC]

[6-8] *opposite below*
DOUGLAS RESIDENCE, PATIO.
[CHARLES KROBECK; EDA, UCB;
c. 1953;]

[6-9] *below*
**DOUGLAS RESIDENCE,
PLAN AND ELEVATION SHOWING
THE PROPOSED SECOND STORY,
1962.**
[EDA, UCB]

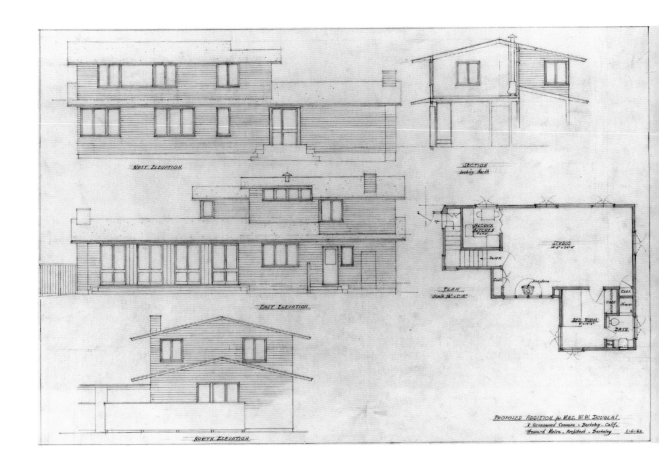

Blaisdell Residence

9 Greenwood Common, 1953

Client:
Thomas C. and Catherine M. Blaisdell

Architect:
Henry Hill

Landscape Design:
Henry Hill

Built on a flat lot, the Blaisdell residence displays the open planning typical of Henry Hill's designs. Long and low, with a flat roof that extended over the wall to provide shade, the design also reflects Hill's fearless use of color and texture both internally and on the exterior [figure 7-1]. Although all the façades of the house use both horizontal and vertical elements, the overall sweep of the design is horizontal.

Representative of Californian modernism, the courtyard—or outdoor living room—is literally the center of the structure. Three fully glazed walls enclose the paved courtyard to frame spectacular views of the Golden Gate Bridge [figure 7-2].

In 1951 Catharine Maltby and Thomas Blaisdell moved to Berkeley where he assumed his position as professor of political science and director of the Bureau of International Relations. Blaisdell was a central figure in the huge expansion of the social sciences on the Berkeley campus as well as in organizing research and programs in the field of international relations. It was in this capacity that he may have come to know William Wurster during a period when Wurster was expanding the architecture curriculum to include social and cultural factors as well as the research interests of the department.

Hill knew both Wurster and Esherick professionally and was one of nine local architects and landscape architects who contributed to a 1949 article in the *Architectural Record* entitled, "Is There a Bay Area Style?"[166] Hill's contribution paid particular homage to Wurster, crediting him for single-handedly "pioneering residential

[7-1]
HENRY HILL, BLAISDELL RESIDENCE, GREENWOOD COMMON, BERKELEY, 1953.
[MORLEY BAER; EDA, UCB]

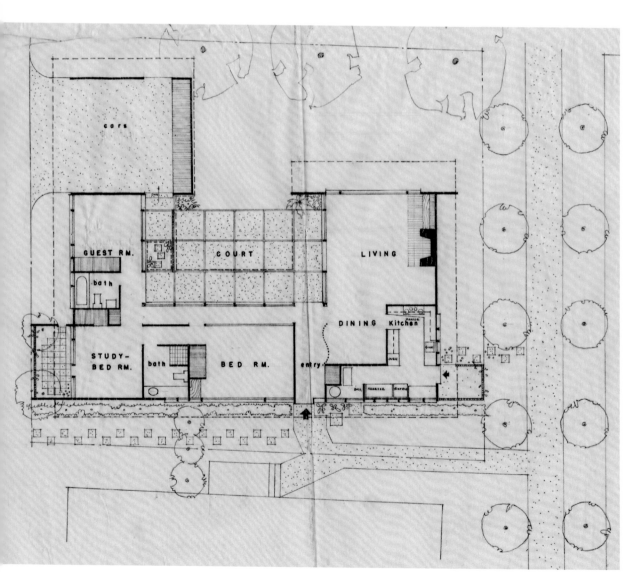

GUEST RM.

bath

COURT

LIVING

STUDY-
BED RM.

bath

BED RM.

entry

DINING

Kitchen

cars

design that expresses the honesty of ... wood frame, and contemporary living." Eight of the nine contributors refused to acknowledge a regional style, a stance that Hill also assumed: "We are not working in a 'style,'" he asserted, "we are working in honesty in our beliefs."[167]

The building permit for the Blaisdell house was signed in December 1952 and construction began the following month. Within weeks Hill was fighting with the building inspector over construction techniques, among them the quantity of plywood necessary for wind and earthquake bracing. In the end they compromised on "half the amount of plywood he had called for and twice as much as I had figured."[168]

Hill was firmly committed to the use of wood and interested in the ways it could be used and finished. In a talk to the National Lumber Manufacturers Association in 1959, Hill defined the wall "as a screen to define ... solid, void, flexible, obscure, grill, or even as a curtain of glass. And the architect's structure delineates this space and its human use." He claimed "wood is inherently a vital and living material and must be treated with dignity for there is no apology."[169] Applying this philosophy to the Blaisdell residence, Hill painted the plywood panels of the fence and exterior walls different shades of blue, mixing the wooden units with clear and opaque glass.

Entire ceilings, overhangs, and fascia board were copper-colored; the trim was stained brown and the front door painted red for a contrasting highlight [figure 7-3].[170] A freestanding screen of oak poles defined the dining room and directed movement toward the living room. Hill later used a similar device—in this case, a vertical

wooden screen—in his Walkup House of 1956 [figures 7-4, 7-5].

Abundant light is a particularly striking characteristic of the house. Every room in the house possessed full-height windows, doors, and even walls that collected light from the central paved court. Constructed on a concrete slab, with radiant heating throughout the structure, the plan allowed for an open flow of public space both inside and out.

The kitchen and living room occupy the north part of the house. Curiously, the kitchen was given an unobstructed view to the Common, whereas views from the living room were directed toward the distant Golden Gate Bridge. The master bedroom traded privacy for the borrowed view through a glass wall opening to the courtyard [figure 7-6]. In the Walkup residence, Hill again used the device of a glazed hallway to provide light and a feeling of openness. A hall separated the master bedroom from the study—which overlooked a private garden to the south—and provided a necessary retreat when Mr. Blaisdell was working [figure 7-7].[171] This arrangement was later transformed into a suite in which each of the Blasidells had their own bedroom joined by the hall and a shared bathroom. The program also required a bedroom/study with a separate entry for evening seminars and included provisions for preparing snacks. Having older children, this space also encompassed a guest unit, separated from the main house by a sliding door [figure 7-8].

Hill imbued his design with spirited colors from the very beginning of the Blaisdell project. The Blaisdell fireplace brick—"Coral" Roman brick (a pinkish tan)—was supplied by the

[7-2]
BLAISDELL RESIDENCE,
FLOOR PLAN c. 1952.
[EDA, UCB]

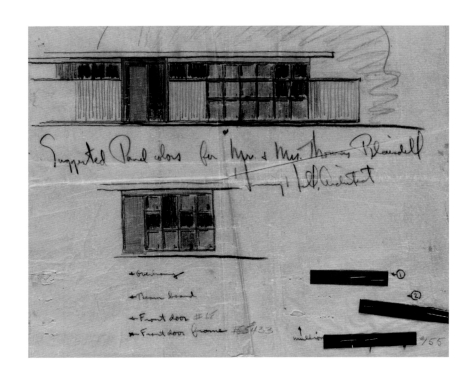

Suggested Panel colors for Mr. & Mrs. Thomas Blaisdell

← Greinary
← Beam board
← Front door #68
← Front door frame #5433

mullion

#55

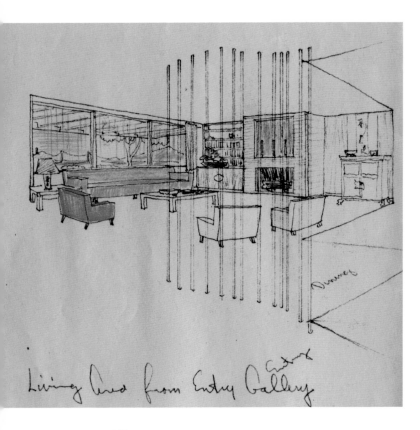

Living Area from Entry Gallery

[7-3] *opposite above*
**BLAISDELL RESIDENCE,
EAST ELEVATION WITH COLOR
SAMPLES, c. 1952.**
[EDA, UCB]

[7-4] *opposite below left*
**BLAISDELL RESIDENCE,
INTERIOR DETAILS, c. 1952.**
[EDA, UCB]

[7-5] *opposite below right*
**HENRY HILL, WALKUP RESIDENCE,
SCREEN WALLS.**
[EDA, UCB]

[7-6]
**BLAISDELL RESIDENCE,
GLAZED HALLWAY AND
COURTYARD, c. 1954.**
[MORLEY BAER; EDA, UCB]

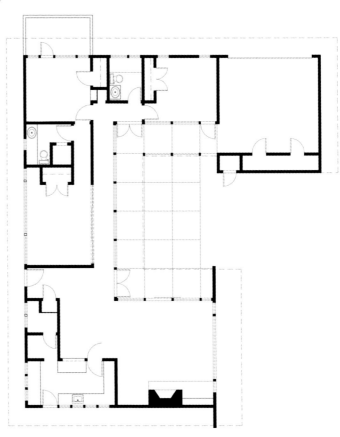

[7-7]
BLAISDELL RESIDENCE, OFFICE, c. 1954.
[MORLEY BAER; EDA, UCB]

[7-8]
BLAISDELL RESIDENCE, FLOOR PLAN.
[MATTHEW GÜEREÑA, 2008]

[7-9] *opposite*
BLAISDELL RESIDENCE, INTERIOR VIEW OF LIVING ROOM, c. 1954.
[MORLEY BAER; EDA, UCB]

noted terracotta manufacturer Gladding McBean. He specified that the floors be constructed of colored concrete and provided the contractor with the precise paint colors for most of the interior surfaces [figure 7-9].[172] Hill also designed the garden and assisted with the interior furnishings, and in February 1954 he wrote to Mrs. Blaisdell about sources for Danish furniture. The letter with attached paint chips illustrates Hill's ongoing concern with the qualities of the house, as he again provided color samples when the Blaisdells repainted their house in 1962 [figure 7-10].

Hill corresponded with Wurster as the Blaisdell project progressed. He informed him which contractor had been hired and when construction would begin.[173] An unsigned 1953 letter, likely from Wurster, includes comments on the "charm and delight of the Blaisdell house," how "it fits the location beautifully," and that "as a plan it is a knockout."[174]

The gardens were planned concurrently with the house and consisted of three areas: the walkway and entrance on the east, the paved courtyard and lawn bordered by trees and shrubs, and the small garden outside Mr. Blaisdell's studio. In February 1952, as Hill developed the planting plan for the walkway, he expressed his displeasure to Mrs. Blaisdell with what he believed to be an unjustified attack on the "reality" of his plan. Copies were sent to Howard Moïse and Mrs. Douglas, with whom the Blaisdells shared the walk. Hill hoped that all parties could resolve their disagreement.[175] The source of the dispute is unclear, but some aspect of the planting was undoubtedly prob-

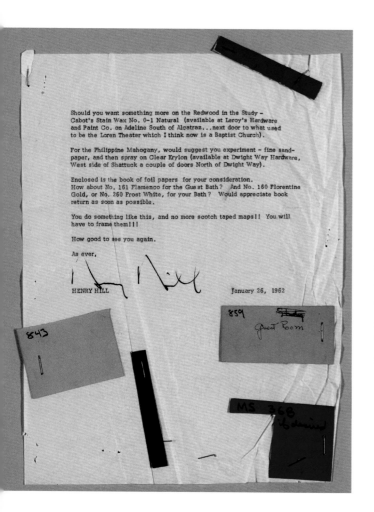

lematic. The plan indicated a four-foot-wide
concrete path leading from the Common,
which divided asymmetrically into a V with
one leg leading to the Blaisdell's door and the
other to the Douglas house. Beyond the fork, the
center tree of a group of three sits on the property line. Perhaps it was Hill's placement of the
tree on the Douglas lot that gave rise to the
problem, perhaps not. The remainder of the
plan positioned shrubs against the east side of
the house, and two rows of staggered stepping
stones and numerous climbing plants —
including wisteria and clematis—completed
the scheme [figure 7-11].

The patio, accessible from every room of
the house, completed the rectangular figure.
Hill's garden design, set in the northeast corner
of the garden, repeated the U-shape of the
house, separated from the Common by a low
range of flowering shrubs [figures 7-12, 7-13].
Sometime later, a fence was installed to provide
a nonporous edge between the lawn and the
Common's walkway. Hill also designed a simple,
mostly paved garden outside the studio.

Henry Hill was forty when he accepted the
Blaisdell commission, which arrived just prior
to the remodeling of lot 7 for Morley Baer. He
had established his own office in San Francisco
in 1948 after working as a draftsman and asso-

[7-11]
BLAISDELL RESIDENCE, DETAIL OF
ENTRANCE PLANTING, NO DATE.
[EDA, UCB]

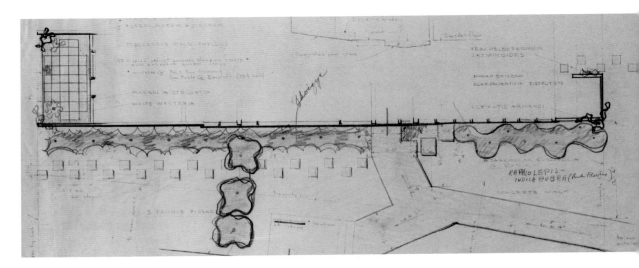

ciate partner with John E. Dinwiddie (1936–1942) and as a partner in Mendelsohn, Dinwiddie & Hill (1946–1948). It was while he was working on the Greenwood Common commissions that his career received increased professional recognition. Hill believed that the architect's expression should be characterized by a fundamental simplicity; that good design demanded a complete balance of site, program, and budget; and that compromise must develop from the honest exchange between two human beings: the professional and the owner.[176]

It may be that this house, initially built as a part of Greenwood Common, has seen the most significant changes to its original design. In keeping with the aesthetic of their times, subsequent owners wanted an interior that was entirely white. To achieve this, they covered the floor with large white marble tiles, enclosed the brick fireplace with a wooden structure, painted the entire interior white, and replaced the glazed west bedroom wall with a shoji screen. In addition, they replaced the upper kitchen cabinets on the north wall over the sink with clerestory windows. In 1989 these owners attempted to add a second story. The neighbors deemed this proposal unacceptable; they were concerned that building height increases on the south side would cast larger shaded areas onto the Common and they were adamant that the design integrity of the community be preserved. This issue instigated a divisive process that, ironically, resulted in the Common's receiving landmark status. In the end, the remodel was denied and the house was sold to new owners.

The third owner had been a friend of Mrs. Blaisdell's and had frequently dined there. Following the loss of their home to the Berkeley fire of 1991, she and her husband purchased the house. They extended the master bedroom and bathroom to the east by several feet, keeping the walls within the existing roof overhang, and added a skylight. Despite the house's landmark status, these alterations were approved because the three feet had been added to the adjacent room on the east side, when it had served as Mr. Blaisdell's bedroom. The renovations also included the inevitable enclosure of the carport and adding a garage door. The owners made a concerted effort to insure that all work conformed with existing design and materials.[177]

The Blaisdell house captures the essence of midcentury California living. The spaces—public and private, indoor and outdoor—flow effortlessly into one another. The design, constructed of regional materials, carefully sites the house among its natural and planted surroundings and its neighbors, with sensitivity to climate, light, and color.

[7-12]
BLAISDELL RESIDENCE,
GARDEN PLANTING PLAN,
NO DATE.
[EDA, UCB]

[7-13]
BLAISDELL RESIDENCE,
COURTYARD, c. 1954.
[MORLEY BAER; EDA, UCB]

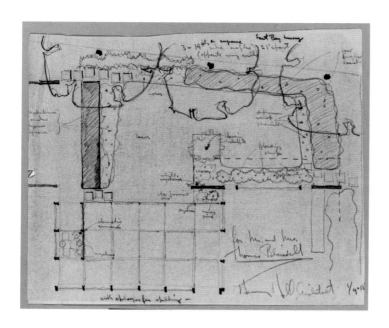

137

Maenchen Residence

10 Greenwood Common, 1953

Client:
Otto J.and Anna Maenchen

Architect:
John Funk

Landscape Architect:
Lawrence Halprin

The profile of the Maenchen residence takes form as a graceful "butterfly" roofline spreading up and outwards from the center of an airy house of glass and wood. The design of the house profits from its narrow site at the crest of a steep slope by capturing the magnificent views of the San Francisco Bay, San Francisco, the Golden Gate Bridge, and Marin County to the north. In its configuration, materials, and landscape it successfully occupies its prominent position and provides a handsome termination to the enclave of houses that comprise Greenwood Common [figure 8-1].

Otto J. and Anna Maenchen immigrated to the United States from Vienna in 1938. Otto Maenchen was a professor of art history at the university; Anna Maenchen, a psychiatrist who had been analyzed by Anna Freud.[178] As educated intellectuals, it is likely that they were aware of the development of modern design in Europe; certainly they sought a functional home executed in a modern vocabulary. Their program for the house required specific spaces for a number of segregated activities, including an individual study for Mr. Maenchen, places for entertaining and sleeping, guest and house-keeper's quarters, and a sleep-playroom for their grandchildren. In addition, Mrs. Maenchen maintained a psychiatric practice that required a home office and study. Their program also required all the principal living spaces to be on one level, with a secluded area dedicated to displaying their collections of books, oriental prints, ceramics, and sculpture.[179] A garden completed their list of desires.

John Funk, their architect, began designing for the Maenchens relatively early in his career.

[8-1]
JOHN FUNK, MAENCHEN RESIDENCE, GREENWOOD COMMON, BERKELEY, 1953.
CANTILEVERED DECK ON THE WEST SIDE OF THE HOUSE LOOKS TO THE GOLDEN GATE.
[MARC TREIB]

[8-2]
**JOHN FUNK,
HECKENDORF RESIDENCE,
MODESTO, 1939.**
[MARC TREIB]

[8-3]
**JOHN FUNK,
MAENCHEN RESIDENCE,
ENTRANCE.**
[MARC TREIB]

He was born in 1908 in Upland, California, and received his bachelor's degree in architecture from the University of California, Berkeley, in 1934 and his master's degree the following year. Between 1936 and 1938, he worked in the office of William Wurster and then established his own practice in 1939. Following the publication of his 1939 Heckendorf House in Modesto on the cover of the Museum of Modern Art's exhibition catalog *Built in the U.S.A., 1932–1944*, Funk's reputation was established nationally, perhaps even internationally. In this book the house, designed for Funk's sister-in-law, was described as an "inexpensive house [with] classic dignity and restraint."[180] Large glass sliding doors wed the living and dining rooms to the garden— the epitome of indoor-outdoor living. In tone and manner, it neatly balanced an uncompromising modernity with a warmth uncharacteristic of International Style buildings—a character that was its primary appeal [figure 8-2]. His house for Mr. & Mrs. W. E. Kirby in Belvedere, California, was included in the 1949 exhibition "Domestic Architecture of the San Francisco Bay Region" at the San Francisco Museum of Art. Its description in the exhibition catalog projects the trajectory of Funk's work later manifest in the Maenchen residence. "A minimum house, overhanging the hillside to preserve the simplicity of the architectural form, is oriented to both view and outside living area.... the imaginative planning and sensitive handling of materials and proportions make the house seem larger than it actually is [figure 8-3]."[181]

Funk's strong social philosophy led him from single-family residences to low-cost wartime housing projects, and ultimately to the 1949 cooperative housing development Ladera, near Palo Alto, designed with the architect Joseph Stein and landscape architects Garrett Eckbo and Robert Royston. Funk began designing a home for the Maenchens that same year, well before the establishment of Greenwood Common. A preliminary study included elevations showing a single-story structure with a long living area set perpendicular to a shorter wing containing the garage and guest rooms. While this plan differs significantly from the house as constructed on the Common, it alluded to a number of similar features—for example, vertical-board exterior siding, a living room with two fully glazed walls, a paved patio, and a full-length balcony. Interestingly, a significant garden feature is not easily apparent [figure 8-4].

Once the property on Greenwood Common had been acquired the design for the house changed dramatically. While the site clearly played a part in shaping the new design— evident in the cantilevered deck that overhangs the sharp fall of the hillside—the origin of other changes, such as the butterfly roof, are less obvious. The so-called "bi-nuclear plan" was a popular strategy in postwar residential architecture, with a plan that diagrammatically took form as an H. In this plan, a central entry —the crossbar of the H—divides private spaces such as bedrooms from those more public, such as living and dining rooms, and kitchens. The roof, however, was another matter and less prescribed than the spatial division of the rooms although the use of opposing roof pitches— the so-called "butterfly" roof—was a common solution. In 1949 Marcel Breuer designed an

exhibition house constructed in the garden of the Museum of Modern Art in New York. It featured a spatially fluid living area capped by an asymmetrical butterfly roof. The project was well publicized and it is likely that the Maenchens became aware of this design either by reading about it or by visiting New York while it was on display.

The architect and clients worked closely to determine the final arrangements for the interior spaces. Drawings illustrating possible configurations record the design process. Certain elements consistently recur in all the proposals, including the full-length deck on the west side, garden areas integral to the living spaces, and a garage at the terminus of the access road on the southeast corner of the lot. Despite minor flirtations with L- and U-shaped plans, the H-shaped plan emerged as the preferred design [figures 8-5, 8-6]. The final plan poised two wings against an entry gallery, with the private rooms to the east (left upon entry) and the public rooms to the west. The voids between the wings were planned as an entry garden and an enclosed courtyard.

The ideas that guided the planning of the Ladera cooperative in 1949 would underlay virtually all the design decisions for the Maenchen house. According to a Ladera sales brochure, this suburb was intended to provide "pleasant, simple living here—today—in California." The text continued:

> We are for indoor-outdoor living. We don't
> want our homes confined to the rooms
> under roof and inside walls. Instead, we
> see our entire lot as our home, planned
> from the beginning as a series of logically

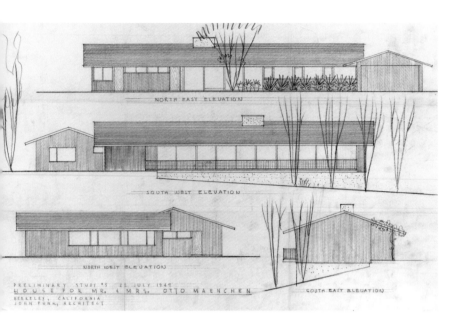

[8-4] *above*

**MAENCHEN RESIDENCE,
ELEVATIONS STUDIES, 1949.**

[EDA, UCB]

[8-5] *below*

**MAENCHEN RESIDENCE, FLOOR
PLAN STUDY, c. 1952.**

[EDA, UCB]

[8-6] *opposite above*

**MAENCHEN RESIDENCE,
FLOOR PLAN STUDY, c. 1952.**

[EDA, UCB]

[8-7] *opposite below*

**MAENCHEN RESIDENCE,
FLOOR PLAN STUDY, 1952.**

[EDA, UCB]

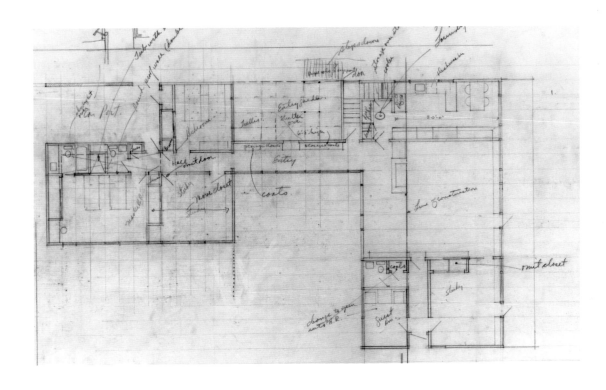

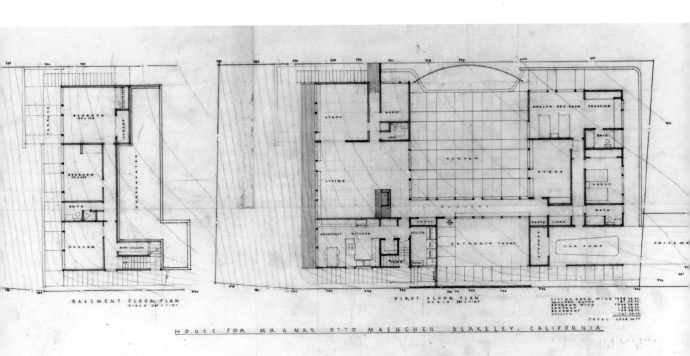

BASEMENT FLOOR PLAN

FIRST FLOOR PLAN

HOUSE FOR MR. & MRS. OTTO MAENCHEN, BERKELEY, CALIFORNIA

connected rooms and areas both indoors and out. We want our "living room" to include the outside terrace; the kitchen to be planned in connection with a convenient service yard; the children's rooms, where practical, to extend into outdoor space for playing.[182]

The dreams of a cooperative community in Palo Alto were left unrealized, but many of the underlying ideas for its houses informed other commissions by the same architects and landscape architects.

Once the Maenchens had committed to the plan, they reviewed the preferred locations for specific rooms and their uses. One study proposed an entry from the common into a hallway that faced a "large square living garden." In this scheme the kitchen faced the Common and overlooked a kitchen garden. French doors in each room opened to the full-length deck, made broad enough to accommodate a range of family activities. An enclosed porch served as a transition area between the living room and the courtyard. The east wing contained a bedroom, study, and guest room—all faced east onto a sheltered "bedroom" garden protected by the garage to the south.

A second study contained many elements of the final plan. It eliminated a porch from the courtyard, as well as the kitchen and bedroom gardens. Instead two outdoor spaces, one defined by a sweeping curve, were centered between two wings of equal length [figure 8-7]. In this plan the gallery was pushed back to the south with floor-to-ceiling glass that revealed the gardens on both sides. The study still faced the Common, and the living room, now graced

[8-8]
MAENCHEN RESIDENCE, GLAZED GALLERY LINKING BEDROOM AND LIVING WINGS.
[MARC TREIB]

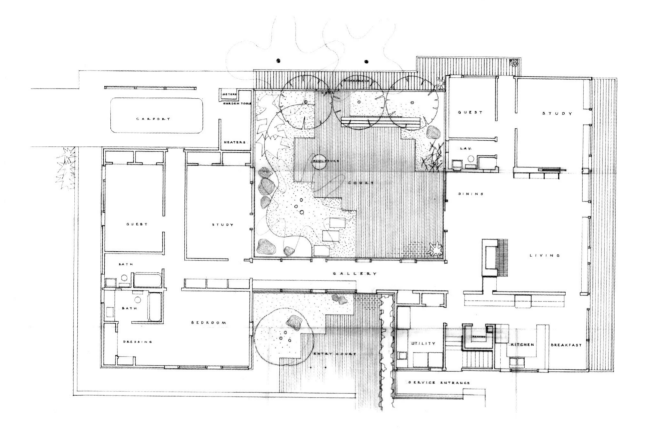

Labels within the floor plan:

CARPORT

METERS
GARDEN TOOLS

HEATERS

GUEST

STUDY

BATH

BATH

DRESSING

BEDROOM

ENTRY COURT

GALLERY

COURT

GUEST

STUDY

LAV.

DINING

LIVING

UTILITY

PANTRY

KITCHEN

BREAKFAST

SERVICE ENTRANCE

[8-9]
MAENCHEN RESIDENCE,
PRELIMINARY FLOOR PLAN, 1952.
[EDA, UCB]

by a fireplace, was larger, freer, and more open to views to the court and the bay. In this plan the enclosed private garden was relatively small while the large front garden served almost as an extension of the proposed public common. In addition, a guest would need to traverse the length of the house to gain entrance.

A phone conversation in June 1952 led to further modifications, among them shortening the left leg of the H and shrinking the interior courtyard. By September the elements were consistently referred to as the living room wing, gallery entry, and bedroom wing [figure 8-8]. By February 1953 most of the key decisions had been made and the construction drawings were complete [figure 8-9].

Ultimately, the Maenchen house was the only structure on the Common with an entrance that directly faced the communal area. In the final plan, the gallery had been pulled forward toward the entry, gaining a sizable central patio enclosed by the house on three sides and a fence on the fourth. Behind the fence was a narrow wooden deck that allowed access to Mrs. Maenchen's office from the end of the Common's southern access road. The living and dining wing was cantilevered over the western slope with a deck accessible from the office, the living room, and the kitchen, which now looked onto the Common. To protect the deck from the summer sun and winter rain, the roof on the west side ended in a four-and-a-half-foot overhang [see figure 8-1].

The family wing housed the master bedroom, bathrooms, grandchildren's room, and Professor Maenchen's study [figure 8-10]. Almost miraculously, it is possible to see the Golden Gate from his study, testifying to Funk's skill in handling the large glass areas and shading necessary to maintain a transparency through the garden and living room [figure 8-11]. Guest room, housekeeper's quarters, and a wine cellar occupied the lower level. The exterior was comprised of vertical, one-by-four, redwood tongue-and-groove siding. Redwood was also the material of choice for the gutters, the retaining wall, and the courtyard fence. The windows doorjambs and sills were all built in Douglas fir.

The interior of the house epitomized the informal elegance of the postwar California modern home. White-birch plywood panels, their grain set vertically, lined the living room, adding a warmth unachievable with the white plaster surfaces preferred by many modernists. Birch throughout reinforced the sense of unity within the living areas: it was used for the bookshelves, cabinet doors, and all casework as well as for the kitchen cabinets and the walls of Mrs. Maenchen's study. The "common red brick" of the living room fireplace complemented the warmth of the light reddish-brown birch walls [figure 8-12].[183]

During their residency, the Maenchens applied for a number of permits to make changes to their house. These included a 1961 effort to allow Mrs. Maenchen to use her office for the psychological evaluation of patients. The request generated bureaucratic concern as to whether that use would conflict with the area's residential zoning. Although the Berkeley Permit Department objected, she nevertheless was granted permission to undertake the necessary modifications; an office in another location would accommodate

[8-10]
MAENCHEN RESIDENCE,
FLOOR PLAN.
[MATTHEW GÜËREÑA, 2008]

a larger percentage of her practice.[184] In response to her application for an "in-law" unit for a live-in caretaker, she was informed that such a permit was unnecessary because that type of living arrangements did not require significant changes to the original guest quarters.[185] Like other residents of the Common, the Maenchens also converted a covered carport to an enclosed garage, but not until 1994—much later than their neighbors.[186]

Funk collaborated with the landscape architects Lawrence Halprin, and Eckbo, Royston & Williams on many of the residences he designed during the late 1940s and early 1950s. According to Halprin he received the Maenchen commission as a result of his friendship and prior collaborations with Funk.[187] It was understood by all parties that the two would work closely to integrate the house and garden areas, and that the planted areas would provide the peacefulness and feeling of a Japanese garden.[188] For the specific landscape elements, however, the Maenchens worked on their garden directly with Lawrence Halprin, accomplishing what exists today in two stages.

In effect, Halprin designed two gardens for lot 10: the entrance garden that serves as the transition between the Common and the front door, and the more intimate courtyard garden [figure 8-13]. The initial plans for both gardens relied heavily on brick paving with planting areas relegated to the edges. The entrance garden is comprised of a geometric border of azalea and agapanthus framing an off-center birch tree and tree fern as their vertical counterpoints. A climbing vine along the

[8-11] *opposite*
MAENCHEN RESIDENCE.
VIEW OF THE COURTYARD FROM THE LIVING ROOM, FACING EAST.

[MORLEY BAER; EDA, UCB]

[8-12] *below*
MAENCHEN RESIDENCE, DINING ROOM.
[MARC TREIB]

west façade extended beyond the wall to screen a service yard west of the entrance.

An asymmetrical brick patio graced by a sculpture pedestal covered nearly half of the space of the interior courtyard. Bamboo, a few large rocks, grass, and river stones defined the southwest corner. The east side of the courtyard comprised three distinct zones. In the final design the curve of a lawn area changed from the biomorphic shape shown in an early sketch to a sweeping arc, but both designs contrast the sharp edge of the geometric brick patio with the planted area. Carefully placed rocks and stepping stones supported movement from the entry and through the garden [figures 8-14, 8-15].

As noted above, the Maenchens were very involved with the garden's design from the beginning. In a detailed letter sent from Lake Tahoe in July 1953, Otto Maenchen raised numerous issues, such as whether there would be enough colors for Mrs. Maenchen who likes them and would she have cut flowers for her study; whether plant heights would obstruct the views; whether a cement terrace under the Monterey pines might be easier to keep clean than one with a gravel; and a concern that the grass might not mitigate the angularity of the patio so was there a way to make it look less severe? He also suggested that the wooden bridge leading to Mrs. Maenchen's study be widened so that it looked less like a tube; cited specific plantings such as a preference for vines; suggested the placement of planter boxes; and enclosed a list of plants in their present garden "taken down from memory."[189]

[8-13]
**MAENCHEN RESIDENCE,
ENTRY WAY, c. 1954.**
[DARROW M. WATT; EDA, UCB]

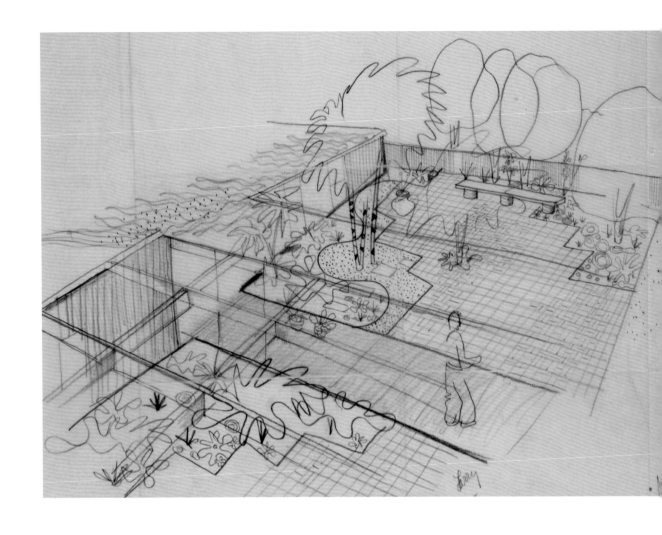

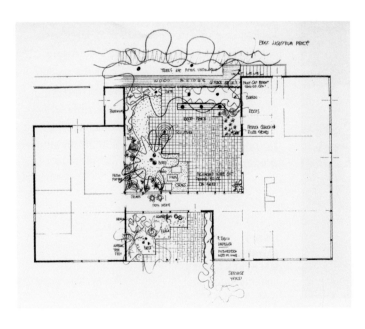

[8-14]
LAWRENCE HALPRIN,
MAENCHEN GARDEN,
PERSPECTIVE STUDY, NO DATE.
［EDA, UCB］

[8-15]
MAENCHEN GARDEN,
FLOOR PLAN WITH GARDEN,
NO DATE.
［AA, UP］

The Maenchens' interaction with their landscape architect illustrates the occasional difficulties of working with home gardeners. No detail seemed too small for their notice or comment. They relayed information from Funk and suggested that Halprin visit a shop on Post Street to see the sculpture recently purchased for the garden court and to talk to the proprietor about large pots he could acquire for them. They also wondered whether Halprin's reasons for placing the retaining wall inside the property were practical or aesthetic— expressing their concerns that "if practical we would feel strongly for having the wall on the property line and planting next to the path way but if you think it would look better the way you suggested."[190]

They went so far as to enclose a list of climbing vines given to them by a friend and asked Halprin to check off the kinds he would consider so that they could visit a nursery to "get acquainted with [all] the plants we have not met yet." In addition, they politely requested that he recommend a nursery where this visit could take place and continued with an expression of their concern with plant heights and their impact on the neighbors' views, the severity of the grass line, and the pattern of the brick.

By October 1953 house construction had progressed to the point where Mrs. Maenchen felt laying brick and replacing soil in the garden could begin that November. Two contractors were selected by the owners, one for the paving and infrastructure and one for supplying the plants. The process proceeded smoothly and the following summer Anna Maenchen sent Halprin a note letting him know that "our little garden is all planted and that we are very

[8-16]
**LAWRENCE HALPRIN,
MAENCHEN GARDEN.**
LOOKING SOUTHEAST.
[DARROW M. WATT; AA, UP]

happy with it. It is good to have a large brick area in the patio, as you suggested...and the flowers on top of the retaining wall instead of below as we [had] wanted them."[191]

During the next few years there the Maenchens discussed a number of adjustments with Halprin but the most significant change to their garden began in November 1955 with their desire to have a fishpond by the library door. Through Mr. Maenchen's professional involvement with art and their awareness of prewar Viennese culture, one can infer that the Maenchens remained informed about the art and design movements of the day. Like Breuer's "House in the Museum Garden," which may have inspired their house design, the Museum of Modern Art's Japanese exhibition house and garden by the architect Junzo Yoshimura (1953–1954) may have inspired the Maenchens to redesign their central court to feature a Japanese-inspired pool and a platform to complement their collection of bonsai [figure 8-16].[192]

Work on the pond project began in January 1957 with its final shape still under discussion. Organic and sinuous, energized by a single jet, Halprin's pond design featured carefully selected and placed rocks (several specified as moss-covered) nestled into a mound along its southwestern edge [figure 8-17]. The completed project—with its quiet polymorphic basin, Japanese maples, and statue of Buddha—was published in Sunset magazine the following April.[193] The author exclaims that exemplary gardens like this don't just happen, they result from creativity, attention to detail, and a close working relationship between designer and client.

[8-17]
MAENCHEN GARDEN,
JAPANESE POOL STUDY, c. 1957.
[AA, UP]

In 1959, Funk designed a second house for the Maenchens, probably a rental unit intended for lot 11. Smaller than the first house, it too was covered with vertical redwood siding and had west-facing decks. Funk's drawings show two proposed designs that expand the ground floor space with a loft, or partial second floor that used sliding shoji screens for privacy [figure 8-18]. The principal difference between the two schemes was the position of the fireplace. A two-car garage beneath the living quarters facing Le Roy Avenue profited from the slope.

Like the house higher on the Common, one scheme featured a balcony that ran the length of the glazed west façade, with a roof line sloped to echo the grade of the hill. In the second scheme the slope of the roof was set symmetrically, with a smaller balcony centered on its west façade [figures 8-19, 8-20].

It is the Maenchen house one pictures when imagining Greenwood Common. Its iconic representation of regional modernism—integrating interior and exterior spaces in conjunction with the use of local materials and a climate-reflecting lifestyle—captures the fundamental elements of the Second Bay Region Style.

[8-18]
JOHN FUNK,
MAENCHEN HOUSE, UNBUILT
PROJECT FOR LOT 11, SCHEME A,
INTERIOR PERSPECTIVE, 1959.
[EDA, UCB]

[8-19]
MAENCHEN HOUSE, UNBUILT
PROJECT FOR LOT 11, SCHEME A,
PERSPECTIVE VIEW, 1959.
[EDA, UCB]

[8-20]
MAENCHEN HOUSE, UNBUILT
PROJECT FOR LOT 11, SCHEME B,
PERSPECTIVE VIEW, 1959.
[EDA, UCB]

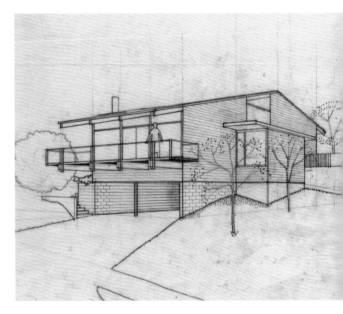

Notes

INTRODUCTION

1 Bubblestone was a new low-cost fire-resistant, lightweight, air-enhanced concrete. Maybeck hung burlap bags saturated with bubblestone as shingles on wires fastened between wooden posts.

2 Marc Treib and Dorothée Imbert, *Garrett Eckbo: Modern Landscapes for Living*, Berkeley: University of California Press, 1997.

3 "Six Moon Hill," *Architectural Forum* 74, June 1941, pp. 382-393; Ken Tadashi Oshima, "The Modern House in the Postwar Period Part 3: Building Utopia at Six Moon Hill," *Architecture and Urbanism* 6, 1997, pp. 6-9.

4 Civic Association of Hollin Hills, 2008, *Hollin Hills, A Modern Historic Community*, retrieved January 2009 from http://www.hollinhills.org/NationalRegister/index.php

5 Robert Winter describes the first bungalow court in Pasadena, built in 1909, as eleven bungalows around a central court. Robert Winter, *The California Bungalow*, Los Angeles: Hennessey & Ingalls, 1980, p. 60.

A planned unit development (PUD) has a number of definitions ranging from a clustering of residential land uses providing public and common open space to a designed grouping of varied and compatible land uses such as housing, recreation, commercial centers and industrial parks all within one contained development or subdivision. The origins of PUDs in the United States in the second half of the twentieth century can be traced to British movements following World War II. British new towns addressed industrial elements prior to initial building, whereas American PUDs typically sought industrial development after residential areas had been developed. The first evidence of PUD zoning in America was created by Prince Georges County, Maryland, in 1949. Other postwar American PUDs such as the Levittowns and Park Forest were often developed within the orbits of larger metropolitan centers.

GREENWOOD COMMON BIOGRAPHY

6 The College of California, located in Oakland was established in 1855; the campus was dedicated in 1860. Beginning in 1857 the college acquired farmland about five miles north as a more suitable location for an institution of higher learning. The trustees continued to purchase parcels adjacent to the northern site and subdivided them for residential and commercial use. The expected profits from the land sales were to pay for the relocation of the college.

7 University of California History Digital Archives, http://sunsite.berkeley.edu/uchistory/general_history/index.html

8 The Morrill Land Grant College Act provided for grants of federal lands to states, which could use income from the sale of public property to support the operations of public universities.

9 Charles Wollenberg, 2002, *Berkeley, A City in History*, Berkeley: Berkeley Public Library, retrieved January 2009 from http://www.berkeleypubliclibrary.org/system/historytext.html

10 Robert Judson Clark, *Roma Pacifica: The Phoebe Hearst International Architectural Competition and the Berkeley Campus, 1896-1930*, retrieved September 2008 from the University of California Digital History Digital Archives, http://sunsite.berkeley.edu/uchistory/archives_exhibits/online_exhibits/romapacifica/partii.html

11 Susan Dinkelspiel Cerny, *Berkeley Landmarks: An Illustrated Guide to Berkeley California's Architectural Heritage*, Berkeley: Berkeley Architectural Heritage, 2001, p. 238.

12 Charles Keeler, *The Simple Home*, Santa Barbara: Peregrine Smith, 1979.

13 Cerny, p. 264.

14 Following the fire of 1923, Dr. and Mrs. Gray, the new owners of Rose Walk, hired architect Henry Gutterson to design most of the residences to replace those lost in the fire.

15 The houses described are the Frances Gregory house at 1476 Greenwood Terrace, the George Noyes house at 1486 Greenwood Terrace, the John Galen Howard house at 1401 Le Roy Avenue, and the Schindler remodel for Sasha Kaun at 1431 Le Roy Avenue. Maybeck and Howard were among the architects who designed in this area designated as the Buena Vista Historic District.

16 Gray Brechin, *California State Historic Resources Inventory*, September 1977.

17 William W. Wurster, "Greenwood Common," 4 June 1962, William and Catherine Wurster Collection, Environmental Design Archives, University of California (hereafter W. & C. Wurster, EDA, UCB).

18 William Wurster to Margaret Prall, 25 July 1950, Correspondence 1950-51 file, William Wilson Wurster, Dean, College of Environmental Design Records, Environmental Design Archives, University of California, (hereafter Wurster, CED Records, EDA, UCB). At the time Wurster was subletting 2683 Buena Vista Way from Prall.

19 Wurster's life-long friendship with and affection for Sadie Gregory was evidenced by the Wursters' naming their daughter Sadie in her honor.

20 "Fresh Meadows; 3000-Unit Housing Development for the New York Life Insurance Company," *Architectural Record*, December 1949, pp. 85-97.

21 William Wurster to Lewis Mumford, 3 October 1949, Lewis Mumford file, Wurster, CED Records, EDA, UCB.

22 *William Wilson Wurster, College of Environmental Design, University of California Campus Planning, and Architectural Practice*, interviews by Suzanne B. Riess, Berkeley: Regional Oral History Office, The Bancroft Library, University of California, 1964, p. 254 (hereafter *Wurster Oral History*).

23 William Wurster to Frederick Duhring, 18 December 1950, Correspondence 1950-51 file, Wurster, CED Records, EDA, UCB.

24 William Wurster to Carl Koch, 9 November 1950, Correspondence 1950-51 file, Wurster, CED Records, EDA, UCB.

25 "Five Houses in Belmont, Mass. Carl Koch Architect," *Architectural Forum*, June 1941, pp. 382-393.

26 "3 New Houses at . . . Snake Hill, Belmont, Mass." *Progressive Architecture*, October 1946, pp. 52-66.

27 *Wurster Oral History*, p. 257.

28 From a statement by John Funk, Greenwood Common Landmark Preservation Application, Berkeley, 1990, p. 78.

29 Originally a remodel design by R.M. Schindler and renovated by Wurster, the house occupied a long, narrow lot that sloped down from the Common to Le Roy.

30 Wurster, "Greenwood Common," W. & C. Wurster, CED Records, EDA, UCB.

31 DeMars, one of the architects for Wurster Hall and Zellerbach Auditorium, ultimately built his own house at the Uplands development in south Berkeley in 1954, while Arthur Kip commissioned Donald Olsen to design a house for him in 1952 above the Arlington in north Berkeley. Olsen built his own home next door to the Kip residence.

32 William Wurster to Buckminster Fuller, 31 December 1953, Greenwood Common file, Wurster, CED Records, EDA, UCB.

33 William Wurster, memorandum, 3 March 1952, *Records of Greenwood Common, Inc.*, Greenwood Board of Directors.

34 William Wurster, memorandum, 24 April 1952, Wurster, CED Records, EDA, UCB.

35 Ibid. An early idea was to keep the private gardens unfenced. This appears to have changed with the construction of the Schaaf fence in 1957.

36 Articles of Incorporation, 13 June 1952, Incorporation Files, Secretary of State Records, California State Archives.

37 Fredrick S. Wyle, "Legal History of Commonly Owned Areas," Greenwood Common Landmark Preservation Application, Berkeley, 1990.

38 Ibid.

39 An article in *House & Home* presented the Common as a successful example of building quality homes on a small parcel of land while providing a sense of suburban space. "By-Passed Land: New Way to Build Five Houses Per Acre and Still Have Lots of Space; Greenwood Common, Calif." *House & Home*, February 1957, pp. 107-114.

40 Elizabeth Kendall Thompson, "Notes by Ann Birge on a conversation with W. W. Wurster at the time of design of their house, 1955," Greenwood Common Landmark Preservation Application, Berkeley, 1990.

41 Acquiring a Le Roy Avenue address for the residence constructed on lot 12 in the early 1960s required special approval from the Berkeley Planning Department.

42 Frances Burnett, conversation with author, December 10, 2005.

43 Gardner Dailey, "The Postwar House," in *Domestic Architecture of the San Francisco Bay Region*, San Francisco: San Francisco Museum of Art, 1949.

44 Ibid.

45 Notice of Annual Meeting of the Members of Greenwood Common, Inc., 25 September 1953, Records of Greenwood Common, Inc., Greenwood Board of Directors.

46 William Wurster to Mrs. Henry Leonard, 14 September 1954, Correspondence June-December 1954 file, Wurster, CED Records, EDA, UCB.

47 Joseph Esherick, *An Architectural Practice in the San Francisco Bay Area, 1938-1996*, interviews by Suzanne B.

Riess, Regional Oral History Office, The Bancroft Library, University of California, Berkeley, 1996, p. 76 (hereafter *Esherick Oral History*).

48 James Ackerman to Marc Treib, 2004.

49 *Esherick Oral History*, p. 175.

50 William Wurster to Robert Birge, 14 September 1954, Correspondence June-December 1954 file, Wurster, CED Records, EDA, UCB.

51 William Wurster to O'Neil Ford, 27 September 1954, Correspondence June-December 1954 file, Wurster, CED Records, EDA, UCB.

52 Catherine Blaisdell to William Wurster, 15 April 1953, "B" Correspondence file, Wurster, CED Records, EDA, UCB.

53 James Ackerman to Tak H. Sakanashi, 12 February [1957], Ackerman file, Lawrence Halprin Collection, Architectural Archives, University of Pennsylvania (hereafter Halprin, AA, UP). By 1957 Lawrence Halprin had been selected by the landscape committee to design the common areas.

54 William Wurster to Robert Birge, 14 September 1954, Correspondence June-December 1954 file, Wurster, CED Records, EDA, UCB.

55 William Wurster to Robert W. Kennedy, 23 February 1955, Correspondence June-December 1954 file, Wurster, CED Records, EDA, UCB. Robert Woods Kennedy was author of *The House and the Art of its Design*, New York: Reinhold, 1953.

56 William Wurster to Donald M. Gregory, 21 April 1955, Greenwood Common file, Wurster, CED Records, EDA, UCB.

57 The Brode residence addition on the south side was added in response to the effort in the late 1980s to have Greenwood Common landmarked. During this endeavor, it was possible that both sides of Greenwood Terrace would be included in the landmarked area. The owners of 1471

were concerned that should this occur they would not be able to make major changes to their home; they constructed the south wing during that time.

58 When both the houses and residents were new to the Common, landscaping tasks were accomplished by individuals or by groups of residents on "work days." Records of Greenwood Common, Inc., Greenwood Board of Directors.

59 Minutes, Annual Meeting of Greenwood Common, Inc., 1970, Records of Greenwood Common, Inc., Greenwood Board of Directors.

60 From a statement by Morley Baer, Greenwood Common Landmark Preservation Application, Berkeley, 1990, p. 78.

61 Greenwood Common file, Berkeley Planning Department, Berkeley, CA.

62 Ibid.

Name, Lot Number, Purchase price:
Robert Birge, #1, $6,000
Alex Bratenahl, #2, $5,000
Frederick K. Duhring, #3, $8,000
Frederick K. Duhring, #4, $5,000
Sophus Stockholm, #5, $5,000
David Russell, #6, $7,000
William W. Wurster, #7, $4,000
Mrs. W.W. Douglas, #8, $5,000
Thomas Blaisdell, #9, $7,000
Otto Maenchen, #10, $10,000
Otto Maenchen, #11, $4,000
Charlotte Morrison, 12, $4,000

63 James Ackerman to the Berkeley Landmarks Preservation Committee, 19 February 1990, Greenwood Common Landmark Preservation Application, Berkeley, 1990.

THE LANDSCAPE

64 Lawrence Halprin, interview with author, San Francisco, November 30, 2005.

65 Ibid.

66 Ibid.

67 William Wurster to the participants of Greenwood Common, 5 February 1953. Courtesy Daniel Funk.

68 Minutes of the Board of Directors, 23 May 1953, W. & C. Wurster, EDA, UCB.

69 According to the landscape architect Richard Vignolo, who worked in Halprin's office from 1950 to 1972, "Larry was mad for flowering plums." Vignolo, conversation with author, July 10, 2008.

Halprin's suggestions may also have included the gravel on either side of this asphalt walk, the type of "topping," and the width of the walk. He added that his primary involvement until then had been to design and supervise the garden for Mrs. Maenchen and to spend an hour advising Mrs. Douglas. Lawrence Halprin to Morley Baer, 28 January 1955, Exhibit 1, Greenwood Common Landmark Preservation Application, Berkeley, 1990.

70 Ibid.

71 Report of Discussion with Geraldine Knight Scott on Landscape Plans for the Common, 30 June 1955, Notes by James Ackerman, Greenwood Common file, Halprin, AA, UP.

72 Report on Discussion with Lawrence Halprin about the Common, 29 June 1955, Exhibit 2, Greenwood Common Landmark Preservation Application, Berkeley, 1990.

73 Report of Discussion with Robert Tetlow about the Common, 20 August 1955, Notes by Ann C. Birge, Greenwood Common file, Halprin, AA, UP.

74 Morley Baer to Lawrence Halprin, 12 September 1955, Morley Baer file, Halprin, AA, UP.

75 Ann C. Birge to Lawrence Halprin, 25 September 1955, Greenwood Common file, Halprin, AA, UP.

76 Minutes of the Annual Membership Meeting of Greenwood Common, Inc., a California Corporation, 5 October 1955, Greenwood Common file, Halprin AA, UP. Tak H. Sakahashi would construct the paving, prepare the soil, and plant the trees and shrubs. A number of issues were raised throughout the two-year construction period: whether the small parking lot at the end of the north access road in front of the Baer house could hold three or four cars and whether to make the mouth of the driveway where it meets Greenwood Terrace serve as a focus or an entrance. There is no further evidence of these issues being addressed. In the end, perhaps for financial, design, or social reasons, nothing was done to highlight either entrance.

77 Ibid.

78 Ibid.

79 Lawrence Halprin, interview with author, San Francisco, November 30, 2005.

80 Halprin explained that his designing Greenwood Common took place prior to developing his RSVP process. See Halprin, *The RSVP Cycles; Creative Processes in the Human Environ- ment*, New York: George Braziller, 1969.

81 Halprin interview, November 30, 2005.

82 Minutes, Membership Meeting, 29 May 1960, Records of Greenwood Common, Inc., Greenwood Board of Directors.

83 Ibid.

84 Minutes, Greenwood Common Annual Meeting, 19 July 1972, Records of Greenwood Common, Inc., Greenwood Board of Directors.

85 Minutes, Landscape Committee, 31 December 1974, Records of Greenwood Common, Inc., Greenwood Board of Directors.

BIRGE RESIDENCE

86 Donald Olsen, conversation with Elizabeth Byrne and author, Berkeley, August 14, 2001.

87 Donald Olsen to Federal Housing Administration, 27 September 1954, Donald Olsen Collection, Environmental Design Archives, University of California, Berkeley (hereafter Olsen, EDA, UCB).

88 Planner T. J. "Jack" Kent, a life-long colleague and friend of William Wurster, was instrumental in both the founding of the Department of City Planning and the College of Environmental Design at the University of California, Berkeley. In addition, Kent taught with Catherine Bauer Wurster in the planning department.

89 Robert Birge, interview with author, April 22, 2005.

90 Obituary for Arthur Kip, *In Memoriam*, Berkeley: University of California, 1995, http://sunsite.berkeley.edu/uchistory/archives_exhibits/in_memoriam/index4.html

91 Birge interview, April 22, 2005.

92 Donald Olsen to Mr. and Mrs. Birge, 15 October 1952, Olsen, EDA, UCB.

93 Ibid.

94 Birge interview, April 22, 2005.

95 Donald Olsen to Mr. and Mrs. Birge, 6 April 1954. Olsen, EDA, UCB.

96 Elizabeth Birge, interview with author, 16 July 2007.

97 Donald Olsen to Mr. and Mrs. Birge, 1 May 1955, Olsen, EDA, UCB.

SCHAAF RESIDENCE

98 Laura Schaaf (daughter of the original clients) interview with author, June 9, 2008. That Klemmedson was also the architect of the Orinda residence was confirmed in a telephone conversation with Robert Klemmedson in July 2008.

99 Ibid.

100 Ibid.

101 Ibid.

102 The Schaaf project file in Halprin's office was initiated with the receipt of a transmittal letter and revised set of plans from architect Klemmedson indicating that the house had been moved back on the lot, Schaaf file, Halprin, AA, UP.

103 Halprin interview, November 30, 2005.

104 Letter from Jean Walton [Halprin Office] to Mr. and Mrs. Schaaf, 16 July 1958, Schaaf file, Halprin, AA, UP.

105 Lawrence Halprin to Samuel Schaaf, 10 July 1957, Schaaf file, Halprin, AA, UP. This garden, like the Ackerman's next door, was designed by Halprin with the understanding that his office would supervise the landscape contractors on a weekly basis, authorize payments, make field changes if necessary, select plant materials, and supervise their installation.

106 Ibid.

107 Schaaf interview, June 9, 2008. During this interview Ms. Schaaf remembered Halprin being "mad for Junipers."

108 Laura Schaaf, interview with author, July 9, 2007. Rose Street was closed east of Greenwood Terrace sometime in the late 1950s or early 1960s. Ms. Schaaf recalled that Rose Street was closed off a few years after the house was built in response to the death of a child in a traffic accident. It is also possible the closure took place at the time La Loma Street was widened.

ACKERMAN RESIDENCE

109 Prior to the hiring of the historian James Ackerman, architectural history had been taught by members of the design faculty.

110 James Ackerman to Marc Treib, 2004.

111 For more information about the architectural work of Joseph Esherick, see Marc Treib, *Appropriate: the Houses of Joseph Esherick*, San Francisco: William Stout Publishers, 2008.

112 Ackerman to Treib, 2004.

113 Dailey, "The Postwar House."

114 Ackerman to Treib, 2004.

115 *Esherick Oral History*, p. 173.

116 Notes for "New Job," Mr. and Mrs. Ackerman, 3 Greenwood Common, 7 July 1956, Ackerman file, Halprin, AA, UP.

DUHRING RESIDENCE

117 Lisa Germany, *Harwell Hamilton Harris*, 1991; reprint, Berkeley: University of California Press, 2000, p. 179.

118 Lewis Mumford, "The Skyline," *New Yorker*, October 11, 1947, pp. 94-96, 99.

119 In an undated letter Mrs. Duhring wrote: "Dear Mr. Harris, After I had expressed my admiration for the house you designed which was featured in Sunset Magazine—Weston Havens suggested I should write to you about planning one for me." Duhring file, Clark & Buettler Collection, Architecture and Design Collection, University Art Museum, University of California, Santa Barbara (hereafter Clark & Beuttler, ADC, UCSB). Although Mr. Duhring's name appears as one of the owners during the purchase of the property, it appears that Mrs. Duhring was the primary client for this residence.

120 Ruth Duhring to Harwell Harris, n.d., Clark & Beuttler, ADC, UCSB.

121 Germany, *Harris*, pp. 31, 109.

122 Bosley, Edward R. "Out of the Woods: Greene & Greene and the Modern American Home," in Edward R. Bosley and Anne E. Mallek, eds., *A New and Native Beauty: The Art and Craft of Greene & Greene*, London: Merrell, 2008, p. 244. Harris's wife Jean Murray Bangs was an early leader in reviving the careers and styles of both Maybeck and the Greenes.

123 Germany, *Harris*, p. 120.

124 Harwell Harris to Ruth Duhring, 12 August 1953, Duhring file, Harwell Hamilton Harris Papers, Alexander Architectural Archive, University of Texas Libraries, University of Texas, Austin (hereafter Harris, AA, UTA). This letter provides the terms of the agreement and Harris's acceptance of the commission. Although Hervey Parke Clark was on record as the supervising architect for the project, architect Bob Lym of Clark & Buettler worked directly with Mrs. Duhring. This also explains why the records for the Duhring house are contained in both the Clark & Buettler Collection at the University of California, Santa Barbara, and the Harwell Hamilton Harris Papers at the University of Texas, Austin.

125 Professor Walter Hart taught English at the University of California and lived in the former John Galen Howard house at the corner of Le Roy and Rose Streets, which is directly below the Duhring's property.

126 Hervey P. Clark to Harwell Harris, 8 September 1953, Clark & Beuttler, ADC, UCSB.

127 Ibid.

128 Ruth Duhring to Harwell Harris, 19 October 1953, Clark & Beuttler, ADC, UCSB.

129 Ibid.

130 Ruth Duhring to Harwell Harris, 18 November 1953, Clark & Beuttler, ADC, UCSB.

131 William Wurster to Harwell Harris, December 1953, Wurster, CED Records, EDA, UCB.

132 Ruth Duhring to Harwell Harris, April 1954, Clark & Beuttler, ADC, UCSB.

133 Ruth Duhring to Harwell Harris, 4 May 1954, Wurster, CED Records, EDA, UCB.

134 Hervey Clark to Harwell Harris, 16 July 1954. Clark, ADC, UCSB.

135 Harwell Harris, "In Designing the Small House," *California Arts & Architecture*, January 1935, p. 20.

136 Bosley, "Out of the Woods," in *A New and Native Beauty*, p. 244

137 William Wurster to Harwell Harris, 27 September 1954, Wurster, CED Records, EDA, UCB.

138 William Wurster to O'Neil Ford, 27 September 1954, Wurster, CED Records, EDA, UCB.

139 Ruth Duhring to Harwell Harris, n.d., Clark & Beuttler, ADC, UCSB.

140 Harwell Harris to Hervey Parke Clark, 7 April 1956, Clark & Beuttler, ADC, UCSB.

141 Hervey Clark to Harwell Harris, 4 June 1958, Clark & Beuttler, ADC, UCSB.

142 Building permit application, City of Berkeley, April 2000.

143 Thompson, Greenwood Common Landmark Application, p. 42.

144 Harris, "Designing the Small House," p. 20. Harris used this device of having indoor rooms parallel outdoor spaces in the Pauline Lowe house of 1933-34.

145 Ruth Duhring to Harwell Harris, n.d., Clark & Beuttler, ADC, UCSB.

146 Geraldine Knight Scott served as the horticultural consultant to Dan Kiley's office for the Oakland Museum of California, and developed a long-range plan for the Blake Estate and Garden owned by the University of California, Berkeley.

147 According to Scott's oral history, she held a long-standing interest in "Oriental art." In the fall of 1954 she accompanied her friend, painter Chiura Obata, on a two-week tour of gardens in Japan, returning again the following spring. Scott made a study of Japanese gardens and the structures in them which she used for numerous lectures. She designed a gate for Mrs. Duhring upon her return from the second trip. Geraldine Knight Scott, *Geraldine Knight Scott (1904-1989): A Woman in Landscape Architecture in California,*

1936-1989, interviews by Jack Buktenica, Berkeley: Regional Oral History Office, The Bancroft Library, University of California, Berkeley, 1990, pp. 124-129.

BAER RESIDENCE

148 David Gebhard, ed. *The Architectural Drawings of R.M. Schindler: The Architectural Drawing Collection*, University Art Museum, University of California, Santa Barbara, New York: Garland, 1993. The other two Schindler projects in the neighborhood consisted of a remodel for Dondo in 1934 and a remodel and furniture design for Perstein in 1933. He also designed a house for the Dondos in Point Richmond, located north of Berkeley.

149 William Wurster to Mary Rapson, February 1951, Wurster, CED Records, EDA, UCB; William Wurster to Douglas Haskell, 9 March 1951, Wurster, CED Records, EDA, UCB; William Wurster to Harry Bent, 14 April 1951, Wurster, CED Records, EDA, UCB. In the letter to Mary Rapson, wife of Minnesota architect Ralph Rapson, Wurster wrote that they were living "... less than a half-mile north of campus and hoped to build a house soon—just as soon as the land matter [purchase of the Gregory land] can be settled ... In the meantime, because of delays, we are trying to buy a most horrible place which does have a superb view of the whole Bay."

150 William Wurster, memorandum, 22 September 1952, Records of Greenwood Common, Inc., Greenwood Board of Directors.

151 The private/public elements of the landscape and the views played a constant role in the development of the Common. The Baers' deed of property transfer included a clause stating that cutting down trees to preserve the view was permitted, but was the owner's financial responsibility. Records of Greenwood Common, Inc., Greenwood Board of Directors.

152 William Wurster to R. Buckminster Fuller, 31 December 1953, Wurster, CED Records, EDA, UCB.

153 Henry Hill, Presentation "Confusion in Architecture," 18 June 1961, Henry Hill/John Kruse Collection, Environmental Design Archives, University of California, Berkeley (hereafter referred to as Hill/Kruse, EDA, UCB).

154 Building permit no. 2040, June 1953; Building permit no. 3372, March 1955; Building permit no. 3749, October 1956; Building permit no. 4759, May 1961; Building permit no. A422, May 1984, Berkeley Planning Department.

155 Gio Morse, conversation with author, July 16, 2008.

156 W.W. Wurster to Alvar Aalto, 10 January 1955, Wurster, CED Records, EDA, UCB.

157 Halprin interview, November 30, 2005.

158 Morley Baer to Lawrence Halprin, 29 November 1954, Halprin, AA, UP.

159 Ibid.

160 Ibid.

161 "Portrait of a Garden," *Progressive Architecture*, December 1961, pp. 138–141. In a 2006 conversation with the author, the resident of this house lamented the loss of three large Monterey pines that had anchored the southeast corner of the garden/Common.

DOUGLAS RESIDENCE

162 "Modern Background for Collection of Distinguished Antique Furniture," *Daily Pacific Builder*, 8 October 1955.

163 In the 1990s a tall fence replaced the hedges while a large cactus displaced the plantings along the shared walkway.

164 Lawrence Halprin to Morley Baer, 28 January 1955, Exhibit 1, Greenwood Common Landmark Preservation Application, Berkeley, 1990.

165 City of Berkeley Use Permit Application, no. 7033, September 7, 1972.

BLAISDELL RESIDENCE

166 Joseph Esherick recalled that Henry Hill was generally considered "a good architect and a nice guy" by those who worked in the Dailey and Wurster offices, although at times he was also considered a prima donna. *Esherick Oral History*, p. 177.

167 "Is There a Bay Area Style?" *Architectural Record*, May 1949, pp. 92-97.

168 Henry Hill to Thomas Blaisdell, 6 March 1953, Hill/Kruse, EDA, UCB.

169 Henry Hill, "Wood in a Living Architecture," Talk at the Annual Board of Director's Meeting of the National Lumber Manufacturers Association, Washington D.C., 9–12 November 1959, Hill/Kruse, EDA, UCB.

170 Henry Hill, "Blaisdell House," Hill/Kruse, EDA, UCB.

171 Ibid.

172 Henry Hill to Albert Hirshfield, 28 January 1953, Hill/Kruse, EDA, UCB.

173 The low bidder was contractor Albert Hirshfield. Henry Hill to William Wurster, 17 November 1952, Wurster, CED Records, EDA, UCB.

174 Unsigned letter to Henry Hill, 9 March 1953, Blaisdell file, Hill/Kruse, EDA, UCB.

175 Henry Hill to Mr. and Mrs. Blaisdell, 4 February 1953, Hill/Kruse, EDA, UCB.

176 Press release for conference, "The American Home as a Work of Art," n.d., Hill/Kruse, EDA, UCB.

177 City of Berkeley permit application, September 1993.

MAENCHEN RESIDENCE

178 Anna and Otto Maenchen were from Vienna where she studied psychology and history and he studied art history, specializing in Asian art. She taught at the University of California, Berkeley, in the School of Social Welfare from 1942 to 1968. Roland Kaufhold, "Edith Buxbaum (1902-1982): Pioneer of Psycholoanalytical Pedagogy and Anti-Fascist Activist—From Vienna via New York to Seattle, Washington," in Esther Altshul Helfgott, ed., *The Edith Buxbaum Journal*, http://www.edith-buxbaum.com, July 2008. Otto Maenchen joined the Department of Art at Berkeley in 1947 and was the first to teach the history of Asian art in the University of California system. W.W. Horn, P. A. Boodberg, E. H. Schafer, *In Memoriam*, Berkeley: University of California. http://sunsite.berkeley.edu/uchistory/archives_exhibits/in_memoriam/index4.html

179 Joan Pringle, "A Formidable Architectural Challenge Successfully Met by a Berkeley Couple," *Oakland Tribune*, July 3, 1955, Sunday edition.

180 Elizabeth Mock, ed., *Built in the USA: 1932-1944*, New York: Museum of Modern Art, 1944.

181 *Domestic Architecture of the San Francisco Bay Region*, San Francisco: San Francisco Museum of Art, 1949.

182 Ladera sales brochure, n.d., John Funk Collection (2002-1) Environmental Design Archives, University of California, Berkeley (hereafter referred to as Funk, EDA, UCB).

183 Specifications for Maenchen residence, 12 February 1953, Funk, EDA, UCB.

184 City of Berkeley permit no. UP4766, May 1961.

185 City of Berkeley permit no. UPA744, April 1985.

186 City of Berkeley permit no. UP2017, November 1994.

187 Halprin interview, November 30, 2005.

188 Lawrence Halprin to Otto Maenchen, 27 July 1953, Halprin, AA, UP.

189 Otto Maenchen to Lawrence Halprin, 13 July 1953, Halprin, AA, UP.

190 The Maenchens to Lawrence Halprin, 19 August 1953, Halprin, AA, UP.

191 Anna Maenchen to Lawrence Halprin, 16 July 1954, Halprin, AA, UP.

192 Junzo Yoshimura (b. 1908) graduated from the Department of Architecture at the Tokyo School of Art in 1931 and worked in the architectural office of Antonin Raymond until establishing his own office in Tokyo in 1941. He began teaching at the Tokyo School of Art in 1945 and became a full professor there in 1962. Yoshimura's innovative design approach is clearly demonstrated in his residential projects; their unusual qualities of calmness and harmony are best explained by his primary concern for the needs of the people who would live in them. He used traditional materials and techniques and created intimate spaces with low ceilings.

193 "In Berkeley, California: A Garden of Refuge . . . Sheltered by the House," *Sunset*, April 1958, p. 92-93.

PARTY ON THE COMMON, 1993.

[COURTESY OF SB MASTER]

Bibliography

ARCHIVES

Berkeley Planning Department, Berkeley, California, Greenwood Common file

Greenwood Common Board of Directors, Records of Greenwood Common, Inc.

University of California, Berkeley, Environmental Design Archives:
Henry Hill/John Kruse Collection
Joseph Esherick/EHDD Collection
John Funk Collection
Howard Möise Collection
Donald Olsen Collection
Geraldine Knight Scott Collection
William and Catherine Wurster Collection
William Wilson Wurster/WBE Collection
William Wilson Wurster, Dean, College of Environmental Design Records

University of California, Santa Barbara, University Art Museum, Architecture and Design Collection:
Clark & Beuttler Collection
R. M. Schindler Collection

University of California, Santa Cruz, Special Collections, University Library:
Morley Baer Collection

University of Pennsylvania, Architectural Archives: Lawrence Halprin Collection

University of Texas, Austin, University of Texas Libraries, Alexander Architectural Archive:
Harwell Hamilton Harris Papers

BOOKS

Bosley, Edward R. "Out of the Woods: Greene & Greene and the Modern American Home," in Edward R. Bosley and Anne E. Mallek, eds., *A New and Native Beauty: The Art and Craft of Greene & Greene*, London: Merrell, 2008.

Cardwell, Kenneth H., *Bernard Maybeck: Artisan, Architect, Artist*. Santa Barbara: Peregrine Smith, 1977.

Cerny, Susan Dinkelspiel. *Berkeley Landmarks: An Illustrated Guide to Berkeley, California's Architectural Heritage*. Berkeley: Berkeley Architectural Heritage, 2001.

Esherick, Joseph. *An Architectural Practice in the San Francisco Bay Area, 1938-1996*. Interviews by Suzanne B. Riess, Regional Oral History Office, The Bancroft Library, University of California, Berkeley, 1996.

Gebhard, David, ed., *The Architectural Drawings of R.M. Schindler: The Architectural Drawing Collection*, University Art Museum, University of California, Santa Barbara. New York: Garland, 1993.

Germany, Lisa. *Harwell Hamilton Harris*, 1991, Reprint: Berkeley: University of California Press, 2000.

Greenwood Common Landmark Preservation Application, Berkeley: 1990.

Halprin, Lawrence. *The RSVP Cycles: Creative Processes In The Human Environment*. New York, George Braziller, 1969.

Hirsch, Alison. "Lawrence Halprin: The Choreography of Private Gardens." *Studies in the History of Gardens & Designed Landscapes*. London: Taylor & Francis, 27, 2007.

Hyman, Isabelle. *Marcel Breuer, Architect: The Career and the Buildings*. New York: Harry N. Abrams, 2001.

Keeler, Charles. *The Simple Home*, 1904. Reprint Santa Barbara: Peregrine Smith, 1979.

Koch, Carl. *At Home With Tomorrow*. New York: Rinehart & Company, 1958.

Mock, Elizabeth, ed. *Built in the USA: 1932–1944*. New York: Museum of Modern Art, 1944.

Oberlander, H. Peter, and Eva Newbrun. *Houser: The Life and Work of Catherine Bauer*. Vancouver: University of British Columbia Press, 1999.

Scott, Geraldine Knight. *Geraldine Knight Scott (1904–1989): A Woman in Landscape Architecture in California, 1936–1989*. Interviews by Jack Buktenica. Berkeley: Regional Oral History Office, The Bancroft Library, University of California, Berkeley, 1990.

Treib, Marc. *Appropriate: The Houses of Joseph Esherick*. San Francisco: William Stout Publishers, 2008.

Treib, Marc, and Dorothée Imbert. *Garrett Eckbo: Modern Landscapes for Living*. Berkeley: University of California Press, 1997.

Winter, Robert. *The California Bungalow*. Los Angeles: Hennessey & Ingalls, 1980.

Wurster, William Wilson. College of Environmental Design, University of California Campus Planning, and Architectural Practice. Interviews by Suzanne B. Riess. Berkeley: Regional Oral History Office, The Bancroft Library, University of California, Berkeley, 1964.

ARTICLES

Arnold, Christopher. "The Work of Henry Hill." *Architectural Design*, September 1955.

Burge, Kathleen. "Cool Ranch: Built in the 1950s, A Community of Modernist Homes May Be Hip, But is It Historic?" *Boston Sunday Globe*, 2 May 2004.

Dailey, Gardner. "The Postwar House." in *Domestic Architecture of the San Francisco Bay Region*. San Francisco: San Francisco Museum of Art, 1949.

Faust, Joan Lee. "The New Emphasis: Planning the Environment." *New York Times*, 8 August 1965.

Harris, Harwell. "In Designing the Small House." *California Arts & Architecture*, January 1935.

Mumford, Lewis. "The Sky Line." *New Yorker*, 11 October 1947.

Oshima, Ken Tadashi. "The Modern House in the Postwar Period Part 3: Building Utopia at Six Moon Hill." *Architecture and Urbanism* 6, 1997.

Pringle, Joan. "A Formidable Architectural Challenge Successfully Met by a Berkeley Couple." *Oakland Tribune*, 3 July 1955.

——"How One House Stood on Its Toes to Get a View of Water." *Oakland Tribune*, 4 December 1955.

"By-Passed Land: New Way to Build Five Houses Per Acre and Still Have Lots of Space; Greenwood Common, Calif." *House & Home*, February 1957.

"Five Houses in Belmont, Mass. Carl Koch Architect," *Architectural Forum*, June 1941.

"Fresh Meadows; 3000-Unit Housing Development for the New York Life Insurance Company" *Architectural Record*, December 1949.

"In Berkeley, California: A Garden of Refuge ...Sheltered By the House." *Sunset*, April 1958.

"Is There a Bay Area Style?" *Architectural Record*, May 1949.

"Modern Background for Collection of Distinguished Antique Furniture." *Daily Pacific Builder*, 8 October 1955.

"Portrait of a Garden." *Progressive Architecture*, December 1961.

"Six Moon Hill." *Architectural Forum*, June 1941.

"Six Moon Hill: Collaborative Planning Integrates Tailor–Made Houses in Co-Op Subdivision, Demonstrates New Idea in Design." *Architectural Forum*, June 1950.

"Snake Hill: Nine Massachusetts Families, Who Have Made a Success of an Experiment in Cooperative Living, Set a Pattern for Other Groups." *House and Garden*, November 1946.

"3 New Houses at ... Snake Hill, Mass." *Progressive Architecture*, October 1946.

WEBSITES

Berkeley: University of California. *In Memoriam*. Retrieved October 2008 from the University of California Digital History Digital Archives, http://sunsite.berkeley.edu/uchistory/archives_exhibits/in_memoriam/index4.html

Civic Association of Hollin Hills. 2008. *Hollin Hills, A Modern Historic Community*. Retrieved January 2009 from http://www.hollinhills.org/NationalRegister/index.php

Clark, Robert Judson. *Roma Pacifica: The Phoebe Hearst International Architectural 1930*. Retrieved September 2008 from the University of California Digital History Digital Archives, http://sunsite.berkeley.edu/uchistory/archives_exhibits/online_exhibits/romapacifica/partii.html

Digital Sanborn Maps 1867-1970. vol. 1, 1929– Mar 1950, Sheet 15. ProQuest Information and Learning, Environmental Data Resources, Inc. http://Sanborn.umi.com

Kaufthold, Roland. "Edith Buxbaum (1902-1982): Pioneer of Psycholoanalytical Pedagogy and Anti-Fascist Activist—from Vienna via New York to Seattle, Washington," n.d. Retrieved July 2008 from Esther Altshul Helfgott, ed., *The Edith Buxbaum Journal*, http://www.edithbuxbaum.com University of California History Digital Archives. Retrieved January 2009. http://sunsite.berkeley.edu/uchistory/general_history/index.html

Wollenberg, Charles. *Berkeley, A City in History*. 2002. Berkeley Public Library. Retrieved January 2009 from http://www.berkeleypubliclibrary.org/system/historytext.html

Environmental Design Archives Collections

JOSEPH ESHERICK (1914–1998)

The Joseph Esherick / EHDD collection (1974-1) is arranged into four series: Personal Papers, Professional Papers, Office Records, and Project Files. Student drawings, and travel photographs and sketchbooks comprise the bulk of Esherick's Personal Papers. The Professional Papers include professional committee work, jury participation, reports, correspondence, speeches, and writings as well as records of consulting projects such as work with the Sea Ranch Design Committee. Office Records include correspondence, notes, reports, and ''Dead Prospects'' (unbuilt projects and unreceived commissions).

The bulk of the collection, the Project Records, documents the work of Esherick and his partners in the firm of EHDD: George Homsey, Peter Dodge, and Charles Davis. These records consist of more than 400 commissions built between 1940 and 1968 for residential, commercial, governmental, and educational clients. The Cannery, University of California, and Sea Ranch projects are especially well-documented.

JOHN FUNK (1908–1993)

The John Funk Collection (2002-1) spans the years 1929-1988 and is organized into three series: Personal Papers, Office Records, and Project Records. The Personal Papers include drawings and photographs of student work, architectural exhibition material collected by Funk, and photographs of Funk. The Office Records contain clippings and promotional materials about Funk's projects, along with documentation and photographs from architectural exhibitions that highlight Funk's Heckendorf House. The Project Records include manuscript files, drawings, specifications, and photographs of projects designed by Funk between 1937 and 1985. Notable projects include the Heckendorf, Zuckerman, and Heymes Houses; several multi-residential communities such as the Hawthorne Defense Housing project and the Ladera Housing project; and commercial, educational, and medical projects, many of which were commissioned by the University of California for its Davis, Santa Cruz, and San Francisco campuses.

The collection reflects Funk's collaborative efforts with architect Joseph Allen Stein and landscape architects Lawrence Halprin; Eckbo, Royston & Williams; Douglas Baylis; and Osmundson & Stanley; as well as photographers Morley Baer, Ernest Braun, Roger Sturtevant, and his brother, Ernest Funk.

HENRY HILL (1913–1985)

The Henry Hill and John Kruse Collection (2000-2) covers the years 1946-1989 and is organized into four series: Personal Papers, Professional Papers, Office Records, and Project Records consisting of files and drawings, most of them for private residences in the Bay Area.

The small series of personal papers includes mostly biographical information such as resumes, Kruse's student drawings and Hill's small collection of quotations. The professional papers contain a collection of writings by and about Hill and his projects, lectures given by Hill, and clippings collected by him as references. In articles such as "Wood in Living Architecture," "Architecture in the Landscape," and "The Individual in Architecture" one sees Hill's emerging influences. Office records contain a diverse range of materials: client lists and ledgers, internal and external correspondence, published articles and promotional materials highlighting the architects' work, Kruse's master detail drawings, and information regarding Tenex, a product used by Hill in his homes. The project files include records, photographs, and drawings from the buildings and private residences that make up Hill's and Kruse's legacy. Many of their homes are located around the Bay Area, but there are also projects from across the country. Major public buildings include the hiring hall of the International Longshoreman's and Warehouseman's Union in San Francisco and a chapel at the public hospital in Moline, Illinois. Also included in the collection are materials that highlight Hill's early ideas and influences on his architecture, including the use of wood, the natural surrounding landscape, and Japanese architecture.

JOHN GALEN HOWARD (1864–1931)

The John Galen Howard Collection (1955-4) spans the years 1884-1931 and is arranged into seven series: Personal Papers, Professional Papers, Office Records, Project Records, University of California, Berkeley Records, Art and Artifacts, and Additional Donations. Unfortunately, this collection contains no materials pertaining to Howard's service as a professor or as the Director of the School of Architecture. The Personal Papers include assignments and student drawings from his studies at the École des Beaux-Arts, watercolors, pastels, and sketches: and a copy of his epic 1929 poem *Pheidias*. The Professional Papers series is small with the most significant group of correspondence relates to the San Francisco American Institute of Architects "trial" and chapter reorganization. Office Records contain scrapbooks, clipbooks, and a few photographs collected for research purposes.

The Project Records document private commissions and public buildings such as the Alaska-Yukon-Pacific Exhibition Complex, commercial and residential buildings for the Spreckles family, and the Gregory family residences. The fifth series focuses on the planning and design work by Howard for the University of California, Berkeley, beginning with the designs for the Phoebe Hearst Architectural Competition and ending with his retirement as Supervising Architect for the university in 1923.

HOWARD MOISE (1887–1965)

The Howard Moïse Collection (1965-1) spans the years 1911-1964 and documents Moïse's architectural and teaching careers and his personal travels. The collection is organized into six series: Personal Papers, Professional Papers, Faculty Papers, Office Records, Project Records, and Art. Personal papers relate to Moïse's education, Army career, and travels. Professional and Faculty Papers contain reports, speeches, course materials, and reference files. Project records primarily document Moïse's work in the Bay Area; though some early East Coast projects are shown in photographs.

DONALD OLSEN (1919–)

The Donald Olsen Collection (2003-1) has not been processed at the time of this writing. The records held by the Archives include tear sheets, project files, drawings, and photographs for projects designed between 1942 and 2000. It may also include professional papers and faculty materials.

GERALDINE KNIGHT SCOTT (1904–1989)

The Geraldine Knight Scott Collection (2000-3) is arranged into six series: Personal Papers, Professional Papers, Faculty Papers, Office Records, Project Records, and Additional Donations that document her design projects and professional activities through drawings, manuscripts and photographs. The Personal Papers include photographs and writings not directly related to her professional life and six sketchbooks/scrapbooks that document Scott's 1939 travels through Europe with her husband, planner Mellier Scott. Her professional papers contain correspondence relating to projects, organizations, and committees; writings, speeches, reference material, oral histories and interviews. Faculty Papers include records documenting her teaching appointments and correspondence related to academic issues, as well as course materials and examples of her students' work from San Jose's Adult Education School and UC Berkeley. The Office Records include a list of people Scott employed as well as a flat folder of typical details used in her office.

The Project Records document works designed by Scott from 1935 to 1987. The collection includes documentation of her work for the 1939 Golden Gate International Exposition on Treasure Island, the Daphne Funeral Home in San Francisco (1953), the Oakland Museum (1963–1987), and the long-range plan for the Blake Estate in Kensington (1968). The collection also contains many private gardens, exhibitions, professional parks, and commercial and educational designs. Scott collaborated with several Bay Area photographers including Morley Baer, Ernest Braun, Phil Fein, and Phil Palmer, and their work is included in the collection.

The finding aids for all the Environmental Design Archives collections may be accessed through the Online Archive of California: http://www.oac.cdlib.org/

Mailing Address:
Environmental Design Archives
University of California
230 Wurster Hall #1820
Berkeley, CA 94720-1820

Telephone: 510.642.5124
Fax: 510.642.2824
Email: designarchives@berkeley.edu
Website: www.ced.berkeley.edu/cedarchives

Index